THE VICTORIA & ALBERT MUSEUM'S TEXTILE COLLECTION

BRITISH TEXTILES FROM 1900 TO 1937

THE VICTORIA & ALBERT MUSEUM'S
TEXTILE COLLECTION

BRITISH TEXTILES FROM 1900 TO 1937

BY VALERIE MENDES

VICTORIA & ALBERT MUSEUM

First published by the Victoria & Albert Museum 1992
© The Trustees of the Victoria & Albert Museum.

ISBN 1 85177 114 X

Designed by Area. Printed in Singapore.
A catalogue record for this book is available from the
British Library

FRONT AND BACK COVERS:
"SMALL FEATHER", block-printed linen. Dorothy Larcher, 1930s. Misc.2[52]-1934

Contents

6   Acknowledgements

Thanks are extended to Mr Donald King, the former Keeper of the Textiles Department and editor of the original edition of the three volumes *British Textile Design in the Victoria and Albert Museum* and to Mr Takahiko Sano who performed amazing feats as photographer, editorial advisor and translator of the first series. Publications are dependent upon team efforts and many curators, past and present, of the Textiles and Dress Collection helped in the preparation of these books. That they are now re-issued for a wider audience is due to the thoughtfulness of the publishers Gakken, Tokyo; the support of Jennifer Blain and Lesley Burton of V&A Publishing and the diligence of Clare Woodthorpe Browne of Textiles and Dress. Finally, we are grateful to all the manufacturers and designers of the textiles illustrated for permission to highlight their outstanding achievements and for readily given advice and information.

FOREWORD

As to be expected, the Victoria and Albert Museum has the world's greatest collection of 20th century British fabrics which illustrates in detail the diversity of textile techniques, vicissitudes of style and shifts in taste post-1900. It was from this rich and extensive source that the following selection of decorative fabrics was originally made in 1980 for the last volume in the three part series published as *British Textile Design in the Victoria and Albert Museum.*

The 20th century collection has been systematically assembled over the years in a regular and painstaking manner. From the end of World War I to 1932 the British Institute of Industrial Art was officially responsible for collecting contemporary textiles. Advanced design was the basis upon which the fabrics were selected and they were acquired at, or just after, the date of manufacture. In 1932, this task was taken over by the V&A and in 1934, on dissolution of the Institute, its collections were transferred to the V&A. The Museum's collection received another boost when the Manchester branch of the Design Registry closed in the 1960s and registered textile samples which duplicated holdings in the London office, were given to the V&A. Early in the century it had become curatorial practice to establish links with contemporary textile manufacturers, designers, craftspeople and retailers and acquire directly from them, fabrics that were deemed to be original and setting the artistic pace. This enlightened approach and conviction of the worth of current British production ensured the survival of many textiles which would have otherwise been lost without recall. With one or two slight modifications, this practice continues today.

The period since this book was first printed has witnessed a healthy and international burgeoning of general interest in, and serious study of, all aspects of the history of 20th century textiles, with design attracting special concern. This development was aided by the emergence of societies, foundations and protection groups some of which allied themselves to general aspects of 20th century art, design and architecture and other, more specialist bodies, which concerned themselves with textiles. Within the UK, further impetus came from various polytechnics and universities which, during the 1970s and 1980s, introduced design history components to their courses and found ready takers. Playing their part in this resurgence, museums looked at their textile collections afresh and planned and, when possible, implemented new approaches to display and the dissemination of information about these collections. With the economic ups and downs of the textile manufacturing industry and the havoc wrought by two world wars it is inevitable that much valuable information including actual textiles has been lost to posterity. However, it is reassuring that, since the 1970s, some leading textile producers have become increasingly aware of the importance of their records of both the paper and fabric variety and they have appointed archivists and conservators to care for, supplement, exhibit and publish these holdings. Given these positive developments and scholarly advances one inevitably looks askance at a text that, brief as it is, was written in traditional V&A mode over a decade ago. Much could now be added but hopefully this short survey of British textiles, 1900 to 1937 still conveys an idea of the fecundity of the V&A's collection and hints at wider interpretative avenues. Above all, the photographs reveal the visual glories of the collection being the products of a multiplicity of talents, chief of which are the designers and the manufacturers.

VALERIE MENDES

British Textiles

1900 to 1937

Valerie Mendes

Edwardian Traditionalism

British textile design during the first decade of the 20th century has been dismissed, as degenerate, or neglected, because it falls between the high point of the style known as Art Nouveau and the emergence of the next clearly identifiable, and in its turn new, decorative genre. In fact this period witnessed the production of a wide range of patterned textiles which, although not startling in their originality, revealed the constants of British textile design – simple floral repeats and technically superb, woven adaptations of historical designs.

Nurtured in Great Britain, Art Nouveau was taken up with considerable verve by designers in continental Europe and its extreme developments were shown at the International Exhibition in Paris, 1900. By the early 1900s its potential had been largely exhausted but its influence lingered. The characteristic extravagant swirls and fluid lines of floral repeating patterns were abandoned in favour of more rigid stylised flower designs such as the block-printed furnishing, plate 1. This degree of formalisation was an innovation much utilised by, among others, Baillie Scott, who employed similar motifs of upright stems with tight simple florets to decorate his furniture as well as his embroideries. Printed dress fabrics from the early years of the 20th century have rarely survived. They were considered to be *déclassé*, and modish dress decoration was mainly achieved by attachment or insertion of costly laces, application of rich braids and trimmings or by use of suitably luxurious, woven patterned fabrics. The lightweight

dress silk, plate 2, printed with rows of peacocks in profile has a static simplicity in common with the cotton designed by Baillie Scott. Peacocks (and their feathers) had long been opulent motifs favoured by textile designers, but whereas the later 19th century depicted them with considerable linear detail and sinuous movement, some twenty years later the bird was reduced to straightforward but none the less effective blocks of colour.

The name Liberty is irrevocably linked with fabrics, in particular printed fabrics. In the 1890s the firm achieved international success with their Art Nouveau textiles and from 1900 to about 1912 they continued to supply an eager market with modified versions of these furnishing prints (plates 3-8). Liberty had most of their fabrics printed by outside firms, including G. P. & J. Baker, Alexander Morton and Turnbull & Stockdale. They were sold as Liberty fabrics in the London store without mention of designer or manufacturer – only by discovery of signed designs or familiarity with types of cloth used by certain manufacturers can they be fully documented. The six duplex-printed cotton fabrics (designers and manufacturers unknown) come from customer sample swatches complete with labels to facilitate ordering. The printing is of a high standard and the pieces share a fresh quality achieved by the use of clear colours, especially green, against bleached white grounds. The frenetic floral movement of the 1890s is now subdued to gently undulating flowering and leafing vertical stems. More complex alternatives to these well-spaced lucid patterns were created (once again for Liberty) by the free-lance textile designer Sidney Mawson who, after about 1905, had considerable success with finely drawn naturalistic patterns in clear bright colours (plates 9, 10). Other manufacturers adopted slightly different approaches to the rendering of these small-scale, domestic florals which gained popular currency in the years immediately preceding World War I. Newman, Smith & Newman issued a series of block-printed cottons in which semi-naturalistic clusters of flowers and leaves were packed tightly together in ground-concealing repeats (plates 11, 12, 18, 19). Reference to the British Patent Office Design Register has helped to determine the dates of these fabrics. This trade protection scheme (started in 1842) registered cloth samples for design copyright. Each sample (showing at least one repeat) was numbered in sequence and sealed to a document certifying date of registration and holding company. In spite of such precautions it is interesting to note that some manufacturers audaciously continued to copy other producer's work. The block-printed cotton (plate 18) contains an almost direct quote from William Morris's "Snakeshead". Two other notable textile firms (plates 16, 17) used historical pattern structures to achieve further variations on these scaled-down floral designs. Ronald Simpson's cleanly outlined vines sit neatly within an ogee framework, whilst vertical meanders are used to great effect in Turnbull & Stockdale's block-printed cotton. Once again a refreshing quality was captured by employing naturalistic greens on white grounds. Such crisp flower patterns were entirely suitable for rooms furnished in the Arts and Crafts manner. They were not, however, in keeping with the highly polished walnut and mahogany furniture of grand Edwardian interiors, which required sumptuous hangings and upholsteries. To meet this demand, long-established weaving firms provided a full range of top quality plain velvets and silks in addition to ranges of elaborate woven patterns based on historical designs. Foremost amongst such manufacturers was Warner & Sons. They wove lavish silks and velvets for both dress and furnishings, which won acclaim at international exhibitions as well as the patronage of the Royal Family. Sir Frank Warner (who headed the firm) developed in 1912 a range of hand-woven velvets (plate 14) based on the designs of late medieval Italian velvets which he had studied in the Victoria and Albert Museum. These were later patented in 1914. A selection was shown at the British Silk Exhibition,

1912, and one in the Paris Exhibition, 1925, although the regulations had clearly decreed that "mere copies and reproductions must be rigorously excluded". The subsequent Board of Trade report stated that "the magnificent 3 pile velvet had not a competitor in the exhibition"[1]. Another Warner fabric (plate 13) shown in Paris, 1925, also relied heavily on historical patterns. Similar textiles were woven by the firm throughout the early years of the 20th century, particularly for ecclesiastical use. Perhaps dependence upon earlier styles can be criticised as a conservative and unadventurous policy but these reproductions were accurate in their proportions, finely hand-woven and, most importantly, sold well.

"Whitchurch" was woven in metallic threads, cotton and artificial silk – the man-made fibre which came to be known as rayon. The 20th century development of man-made fibres presented new challenges for textile designers and technicians. The viscose process was patented in Great Britain in 1892, though it did not come into general use before the early 20th century. Braid manufacturers were amongst the first bulk buyers of artificial silk and they were joined in about 1910-11 by hosiery and underwear producers. Initially those manufacturers specialising in furnishing fabrics were hesitant to employ the new fibres, but gradually started to combine them with natural yarns to produce patterned soft furnishings which sold readily. Rayon was used to provide bright design highlights, while the other materials supplied the "warmth, softness, resilience and most of the strength"[2].

Embroideries designed and worked with immaculate hand stitching by Mrs Christie continued the British tradition of the naturalistic representation of flora and fauna. Her work (plate 15) has features in common with Sidney Mawson's printed textiles (plates 9, 10) both betraying a close and sensitive study of nature, interpreted in fresh clear colours. The most striking aspect of her embroideries were their contrasting textures, attained by juxtaposing a wide variety of stitches. She encouraged diligent examination of historical embroideries and her publications on the subject became standard works. It is a notable irony that her delicate, finely embroidered panel was completed in 1914, just one year after the defiant abstract designs of the Omega Workshops challenged such traditional attitudes to pattern making.

Break with the Past: Abstract Design and its Influence

The most significant aspects of woven, printed and embroidered textile design from 1913 to 1939 are the changes in texture, colour and pattern prompted by increased mechanisation, the development of man-made fibres, new dyes and above all the designer's revolt against traditional patterns. Textile design became closely allied to mainstream movements in architecture and the fine and graphic arts. The proliferation of printed textiles during the socially and economically troubled period under consideration is due to the fact that textile printing was (and still is) the cheapest and most adaptable method of ornamenting fabrics. The manufacturer William Foxton pointed up this fact by labelling textiles such as the colour print, plate 38, a "modern inexpensive machine printed cretonne"[3]. As we have seen, during the first twelve years of the 20th century textile patterns were, in the main, low key variations on themes current in the 1890s. However, with the appearance of textiles designed and sold by Roger Fry's Omega Workshops, a radically new style emerges (plates 20-26). Clearly influenced by developments in contemporary painting (almost all the members were fine artists) they were far in advance of their time and set a fashion for abstract and geometric pattern. The range of textiles included printed and woven furnishings, carpets and embroideries. Though the press ridiculed their work, a small circle of avant-garde admirers purchased Omega goods. For this daring minority Omega textiles were dual purpose and could be used as dress materials as well as furnishings – the Workshops made ladies' linen tunics to order. Fifty years later young girls similarly were to use bold 1960s furnishing lengths to create tubular shift dresses. The Museum has a waistcoat of "Cracow" (plate 20), a pattern which was actually advertised as a durable tapestry for upholstery. This was certainly the most formal Omega design – its regularity dictated by the loom. At first glance the printed linens appear to be haphazard arrangements of lines and painterly splodges. However, this is not the case, as on closer examination they meticulously conform to repeating pattern rules. They were printed by the Maromme Printworks by an undivulged special technical process aimed at preserving the "freedom and spontaneity of the original drawing"[4]. True pattern freedom was really only achieved when the Omega artists painted with dyes directly on the silks and linens. These revolutionary prints were characterised by their abstract design, bright bold colouring, emphatic black lines and undyed grounds. Defying many traditional pattern conventions, they established fresh decorative guidelines which were taken up by the textile industry when it slowly returned to normal operations after the 1914-18 war.

The period 1910 to 1914 witnessed the beginnings of a change in fashionable colours. Much has been written about the potent influence of Leon Bakst's brilliantly coloured costume and stage designs for Diaghilev's ballet (whose first London performance was in June, 1911). There were obvious repercussions – especially in the fields of textile and dress design. The couturier Paul Poiret jealously claimed to have been the first to set the trend for strong colours. However it now seems likely that both Bakst and Poiret were but precursors of the inevitable movement from pale to violent hues. Aided by a rapidly expanding synthetic dyestuffs industry the possibilities of dynamic colouring were fully explored by British textile designers after 1918. Foremost amongst these were Charles Rennie Mackintosh, Claud Lovat Fraser and Minnie McLeish – all highly skilled designers and colourists. William Foxton printed many of their fabrics. He saw himself as an enlightened manufacturer bringing together art and industry, and he made full use of this notion in his advertising campaigns. Indeed his textiles were some of the most exciting available throughout the 1920s. In his who's who of freelance designers, *British Textile Designers Today* (F. Lewis, 1939), H. G. Hayes Marshall was fulsome in his praise of William Foxton – "No man ever had a greater desire to improve the standards of design in Furnishing Textiles in England (sic). No man ever worked so hard for this end – no man had so little help and encouragement. His only mistake was being 20 years too soon".

Charles Rennie Mackintosh produced a vast number of textile designs from about 1916 to the early 1920s, some of which were purchased by Seftons as well as Foxtons. Many of the designs exist but few of the fabrics appear to have survived. The outcome of his stylisation of natural forms were patterns of waved lines or meanders embellished with gently curved motifs (plates 27, 28). His colours became brighter and harsher, outlined in black. All Claud Lovat Fraser's work, whether it be theatre designs, book and graphic illustration, or textile patterns, was remarkable for its vivid, perfectly balanced colours. Using simple blocks of colour he built up startlingly effective repeating patterns (plate 30). They were as successful at the beginning of the 1920s as they were in 1973 when Liberty issued a range of printed dress silks based on his confident, gaily coloured geometric designs. Professional textile designers have been consistently neglected and many talents have passed unheralded. One such was Minnie McLeish who reached her creative peak in the mid to late 1920s. She had a powerful approach, being especially vigorous in her handling of colour, as is strikingly exemplified by the large-scale printed furnishing fabrics (plates 51, 52). The manufacturer Sir James Morton printed a number of her designs and his instructions to his studio (where one of her sketches was being prepared for production) summed up her abilities: "keep the same bright brilliant colours... and the same wild-looking character in the design. Don't trim and civilise it any more than is necessary for the interpretation on design paper"[5]. Minnie McLeish was also capable of great restraint, as is evidenced in her small-scale geometric design of 1921 (plate 40).

Certain dominant elements, characteristic of 1920s patterned textiles, can be seen in the work of Constance Irving and Gregory Brown, once again free-lance designers who supplied William Foxton. The liberating influence of abstract art as well as a graphic fondness for black are apparent in Gregory Brown's powerful arches (plate 37), while Constance Irving's textiles reveal luminous colours intensified by black outlines and details. Unfortunately, little is known about her career. A typical example of the buoyant, spirited quality of her designs (plate 38) shows a simple vertical stripe, made exceptional by bands of vividly coloured geometric decoration. Balance is achieved in her lyrical "Harebell" design by the interplay of all-over curving floral trails and paired harebell columns (plate 41).

George Sheringham's fabrics were outside mainstream design developments. His penchant for soft colour harmonies and figurative designs betrays a devotion to 18th century pastoral themes. A versatile designer, he could create a misty impressionist floral dress fabric (plate 34), where the forms appear to flow into each other, or render a still-life group of shells and gourds (plate 35) in a bold abstract manner.

At the end of the 19th century and throughout the 20th century, in the face of outside competition, British textile printing and dyeing industries made various attempts at internal reorganisation to boost trade and efficiency and eliminate undue rivalry. In November 1899, an ambitious amalgamation of forty-six printworks (some with spinning and weaving plant) and thirteen merchant businesses – the Calico Printers' Association – was formed. Its deed of incorporation stated "the businesses acquired comprise about 85 per cent of the calico printing industry in Great Britain. The strength of the Association is shown by the fact that it includes nearly every leading house in the trade, and that these supply goods not only to all branches of the home trade, but practically to every open market of the World. The businesses also deal with all sections of the trade and include the production of every description of printed cotton, dress goods, furniture, cretonnes, linings, flannelettes, and also of delaines and mixed fabrics"[6]. In the difficult economic climate of the inter-war period the members of the Association (including many firms founded in the 18th century) retained their specialities and strove to "preserve the tradition and standing of calico printing and to produce textiles of a high standard at reasonable prices"[7]. Many firms encouraged their designers to explore the possibilities of abstract patterns utilising the wide range of latest fast colours, which resulted in the creation of numerous inventive and lively designs. The bulk of surviving Calico Printers' Association production is in the form of registered textile samples. It has been possible to ascertain that they were printed by the Association, though further details about designers or printworks have proved elusive. Valuable records were lost as the Association, battling for survival, was forced to close non-viable works – in 1918 it had twenty-nine printworks in operation but by 1939 this number was reduced to eleven.

F. W. Grafton in Manchester excelled in the printing of particularly richly coloured patterns. The combination of purples, black and orange of the roller-printed trellis, grapes and flower design (plate 31) was entirely typical of their output. This resembles a stencilled fabric designed and printed by Francis Jourdain which was shown at the Paris Exhibition, 1925. It raises the question of influences and there is no doubt that by the mid-1920s French textile designers were leaders in their field. Nevertheless their British counterparts offered adventurous alternatives especially for printed yardage.

Printed textile patterns dating from about 1921 to 1930 can be divided into three fairly broad stylistic categories: patterns with dark, sometimes black grounds, stylised fantasy designs and finally geometric patterns. The formalised floral spray with immense blue catkins of 1927 (plate 56) was an extreme example of the kind of the 20th century stylistic innovation mentioned earlier. Traditional naturalistic representation of flowers (for so long the chief motifs of decorative design) was abandoned in favour of free flowing stylisation often in massed bright colours on dark, even black backgrounds. Innumerable variations on this decorative ploy came on to the market and they ranged from the simple daisy stripe (plate 36) to the more sophisticated roller-print with its Eastern touches of paper lanterns and diminutive birds (plate 48). The latter was prompted by a mid-1920s fashionable interest in Oriental Art. Reversal of this pattern method followed, and in the resulting contre-jour style, dark foliage occasionally enlivened with coloured flowers and fruits was set against a light ground (plate 53). Woven textile designers also gained maximum decorative impact by placing vivid colours against sombre grounds. See, for example, plate 58. Made by Morton & Sundour, it is a double-cloth composed of cotton, fine wool, silk and cotton chenille. The weave was perfected in the 1890s and seen to greatest advantage in the subtly coloured patterns of C. F. A. Voysey. Light yet warm, as well as durable, over the years the cloth had proved its worth, so the firm updated it to suit 1920s taste.

Semi-realistic patterned textiles with nostalgic and exotic overtones had a ready market. Often a framework of stylised trees was employed, beyond which one caught tantalising glimpses of landscaped vistas (plate 54). A particular type of conventionalised drooping tree became extremely popular with decorative artists in the 1920s – probably initially inspired by weeping trees in sets for Diaghilev's ballet. Some manufacturers peopled their peaceful pastoral scenes. F. W. Grafton pandered to nostalgia by placing demure crinoline ladies in their arbours of 1923 (plate 50). Satisfying a sentimental yearning for times past, this figure was a combination of elements taken from well dressed belles of the 18th and 19th centuries. In the 1920s they appeared on decorated surfaces ranging from textiles to china.

Those with a taste for the exotic could purchase textiles printed with tropical extravaganzas (plate 49). The silhouetted palm trees create an elegant linear network over large stylised blooms and tiny white-washed houses. Similarly the British public could escape the gloomy vagaries of their climate in cascading floral fantasies such as that depicted in plate 55.

1920s designers were especially fond of all-over repeating patterns featuring the circle. In its simplest form, but in vibrant colours, it was used to relieve the tedium of a vertically striped furnishing of 1921 (plate 39). Six years later it became the focal point of a daring pattern full of movement, as clusters of balloon-like circles are crossed by barbs (plate 57). At the end of the decade Sandersons printed a far more restful repeat based upon interlocking segmented circles which filled the entire pattern surface (plate 60). Another much exploited geometric device was the oval. This satisfying form appeared in an assortment of guises and on all qualities of cloth, from lightweight dress voiles to hard wearing upholstery fabrics. It formed frames for bunches of bulbous, full blown flowers (again typical motifs of the period – plates 33, 44). F. Steiner (an independent company) issued a furnishing print (plate 32) with fungus-like ovals clinging to tree trunks, as well as a dress voile (plate 46) with all over clusters of oval-shaped berries. Ovals linked the asymmetrical trellis of the printed cotton, plate 43, and they were decorated in a manner which suggested the designer had been influenced by artists of the Glasgow School. The reticulated gourd-like ovals on the dress fabric, plate 42, are in the same class as the segmented oval flower heads on the far sturdier printed woollen plush upholstery material, plate 47. Gigantic ovals within a diamond framework (plate 45) show mass-producers capitalising on the home market for resist and marbled styles. Their roller-printing machinery could imitate the much more laborious hand resist-printing techniques and produce startlingly bold furnishings.

Batik (the hand-printing and dyeing of textiles by the wax

resist method) became enormously popular in the 1920s. The Western centre of this traditional Javanese craft was, naturally enough, in Holland with its East Indian colonial links. From Haarlem it spread to Paris via a most able practitioner and teacher, Madame Marguerite Pangon, who married traditional technique to modern design. Jessie Marion King was introduced to batik in Paris. As well as producing splendid batiks herself, she wrote and illustrated a delightful handbook on the subject – *How Cinderella was able to go to the ball*, 1924-26. The silk batik shawl (plate 59) was designed and executed (1924-26) by Miss Winifred Kennedy Scott. She had studied at Glasgow School of Art and it was likely that she had been instructed by Ann Macbeth and influenced by Jessie Marion King's work. The shawl's resplendent peacocks, lanceolate leaves and colours are typical of the Glasgow School style. Many of these fragile silks have vanished – it was chic to make them into evening dresses or shawls with long, heavy, knotted fringes, which did not improve their chances of survival. At the turn of the century pioneer embroideresses of the Glasgow School adopted a new and bold approach to the art of appliqué. In the 1920s this was evolved further by Mary Hogarth and her associates. The banner they embroidered from a design by Duncan Grant (plate 64) was composed of simple fabric cut-outs, laid down with fairly coarse stitches and enhanced with glistening beads – it had theatrical impact which would have proved impressive in an ecclesiastical setting. This almost defiant attitude towards embroidery was taken up by others in the vanguard, including Rebecca Crompton (plate 71). Her vigorous and at times iconoclastic attempts to revitalise the craft during the 1930s are evident in her publications. Machine and hand techniques and appliqué were freely combined to achieve some of the most important, influential and foward-looking embroideries of the period.

THE ECLECTIC THIRTIES

At the beginning of the 1930s, faced with increasing external price competition, the British government introduced tariffs to protect the textile trade. This had the required effect of boosting home and export markets in addition to encouraging the new wave of young and inventive designers. British textile design of the 1930s has been much criticised and compared unfavourably with production from the rest of Europe. Yet many British firms made significant advances, exploiting as they did the latest techniques and adventurous patterns; artist-craftsmen created top quality work, while numerous sections of the trade benefited from gifted *émigré* industrialists, craftsmen and designers. French design supremacy, so blatantly obvious at the 1925 Paris Exhibition, acted as a catalyst to the British design reform movement which was in full flood by the mid-1930s. Textile production was a vital part of this effort to regain artistic status and markets. Influenced by the fine arts and advanced architectural styles, textile designers explored the possibilities of the abstract but, as we shall see, never fully abandoned the floral tradition. On the whole the British public of the 1930s were well served by their textile industry. The stylistic range of furnishings was wide – from sparse clean lines of modern abstracts to reproductions of historical patterns. The choice of printed dress fabrics extended from pastel-coloured floral Liberty prints to tiny geometric motifs in solid colours on dark grounds .

Modish 1930s dress displayed supple, gently flared lines which followed the body's contours. To achieve this fluidity, dresses were constructed in soft materials cut on the cross and diagonally seamed. Tiny patterns in primary colours with white highlights on dark grounds (black or navy blue) were in great demand and ideal for this fashion (plates 86-88). Slightly larger patterns (plates 83-85) were produced for a more daring clientele. However, the most eye-catching 1930s dress prints (executed in almost luminous colours) were the free and painterly patterns by Alec Walker (plates 79-82).

From the time of their introduction (about 1912) Liberty dress fabrics with small-scale floral patterns became progressively popular and reached their zenith in the mid-1930s. Their characteristics were summarised by this advertisement "The patterns are delightful – small designs with fresh yet soft colours and a piquant something about them that is very young and yet very knowing"[8]. They achieved international fame and were much used for children's smocks as well as adult's dresses. The firm's catalogues illustrated an immense variety of printed dress silks, linens, cottons, and wools, each with its appropriate name. "Runis" crêpe was a successful cotton crêpe (plates 89, 90) but perhaps the best known quality – and one which is still produced – was "Tana" lawn. Some of the dress fabric printing was contracted to outside firms but a certain amount, including handkerchiefs and scarves, was hand block-printed at Liberty's Merton Abbey Works. "Poppy and Daisy" was one of their best sellers (plate 91) and like so many of their floral prints was (and still is) constantly revived, adapted and recoloured to suit current fashions. The quality of British dress fabrics equalled that of their French competitors. At a lecture to the Royal Society of Arts (1941), Ernest Goodale revealed that "British manufacturers of dress materials who were unable to sell them to buyers in this country, frequently sold them to wholesale houses in Paris. British buyers on visiting that city, quite unknowingly bought these British fabrics in the firm belief that they were the latest products of French looms"[9].

A series of cotton furnishings roller-printed by Arthur Sanderson from about 1929 to 1932 revealed a late, but successful development of the 1920s vogue for vivid colours. Particularly startling were large-scale floral designs with flat areas of intense colour (plate 73) and bold patterns based upon horizontal rows of flowers (plates 74-78).

A number of manufacturers, including Sandersons, produced warp-printed textiles (shadow cretonnes) which had a ready market in the early 1930s. The outlines of geometric patterns (plates 66-68) were attractively blurred by this technique. "Alice in Wonderland" (plate 65) represents that important group of British Textiles known in the trade as novelty fabrics. Lighthearted printed patterns on both furnishing and dress fabrics were figurative or composed of realistically drawn, familiar objects. Clothing manufacturers made these amusing prints into summer frocks, beach wear and childrens wear while in the home, larger scale designs were deemed suitable for nurseries and kitchens. Approaching the end of his professional working life, Voysey simply adapted Tenniel's 1865 illustrations for Lewis Carroll's world famous children's book and sold it to Morton Sundour who made it available in six colourways on a practical semi-glazed cotton.

The work of many artist-designers was directly influenced by international styles in the fine and graphic arts. Frank Ormrod's daffodil sprays (plate 63) show the application of Cubist principles to textile design. Gregory Brown was primarily a graphic designer and his tight cleanly outlined textile patterns (plates 69, 70, 72) represent extensions of his 1930s book and poster illustrations.

A change in fashionable colours became evident by the later 1920s and early 1930s. For top-market furnishings a subdued palette was *de rigueur*. Chairing a meeting at the Royal Society of Arts in 1934, T. C. Dugdale said "... we were becoming so anaemic that we dare not flaunt a coloured handkerchief in our waistcoats"[10]. With rare exceptions, (there were a few ardent crusaders against pallid and dreary hues) avant-garde textile designers and manufacturers of the 1930s avoided pure, bright colours. Natural and all shades of beige were safe. Colours were usually dampened by the addition of black or white, and terra-cotta or dark blue were used when strong notes were required.

As the modernist interior became increasingly streamlined with walls and upholsteries in neutral shades, curtains and rugs with striking abstract patterns were acquired by an affluent minority to provide decorative relief and focal points. Marion Dorn (plate 113) and E. McKnight Kauffer (plate 112) were amongst the first designers to emulate the high standard of luxury carpet design achieved by the French. They were joined by others, eager to create appropriate floor coverings for contemporary interiors. In the main, mechanised industry did not support the design reform movement. Setting up a design on a power loom was costly and many manufacturers continued production of proven mediocre lines which guaranteed a regular turnover and profit. However, the Wilton Royal and Edinburgh Weavers were enterprising firms prepared to take risks and make knotted carpets of avant-garde design. Marion Dorn led the field and throughout the period supplied exclusive designs for the Wilton Royal Wessex hand-tufted rugs and power loom carpeting for top hotels, luxury ocean-liners and the homes of the chic and famous. Ashley Havinden's rugs (plate 114) had clear calligraphic designs which were given appropriate names such as "Uccello", "Milky Way" and "Silvan".

The adoption of screen-printing methods was a major development in the printed fabrics industry. The technique afforded great scope for relatively cheap design experiments. Like the block-printing technique, it is a flexible system which does not dictate pattern height nor restrict colours – the two major limitations of roller-printing. Manufacturers quick to realise its potential and screen-printed modern designs on relatively short lengths. Allan Walton was one of the most enlightened printed textile producers of the period. He commissioned a wide range of designs from a medley of top professional designers and artists. Although he made frequent visits to supervise printing, his brother Roger Walton was chiefly responsible for the production end of the firm at Little Green Dyeworks, Manchester. Until 1939 Vanessa Bell's and Duncan Grant's designs (plates 95-98) were screened on linen, cotton and a satin-finish mixture of cotton and rayon which, due to its soft drape, was admirably suited to their free-flowing patterns. Allan Walton gave his public a choice of these painterly patterns or the straightforward geometric designs by H. J. Bull and T Bradley (plates 105, 106). Allan Walton favoured the shining rayon-faced cloth because it intensified colour and reflected light, but other soft furnishing manufacturers were more timorous in their use of artificial silk. It is interesting to compare Frank Dobson's fluid abstract design (plate 104) printed on the soft rayon by Allan Walton, with the more rigid figurative design lino block-printed by the sculptor himself, using printers' inks on a stiff, non-reflective linen (plate 103).

Certain long-established firms such as Donald Brothers and Old Bleach Linen operated both weaving mills and printing sheds and screen-printed goods which in every way equalled the high standards of their woven production. In general terms costs were reduced by use of undyed grounds and complex, many-coloured designs were shunned in favour of well-spaced, drop or half-drop repeats in up to six colours Using this simple formula, surprisingly bold decorative statements were made (1936-38) by patterns such as Paul Nash's "Fugue" (plate 100) and Marion Dorn's "Aircraft" (plate 110).

Many weaving manufacturers ensured their survival by producing 'bread and butter' lines of popular period reproductions, stripes, checks and plains. Only occasionally did they take the economic risk of including avant-garde designs in their seasonal releases. Other mass producers (especially Morton Sundour with their experimental unit, Edinburgh Weavers) were more whole-hearted in their commitment to the contemporary.

A talented group in the industry directed production of outstanding woven patterns. At Warner & Sons, Alec Hunter supervised the hand-weaving of prototypes for eventual power loom weaving which realised the full potential of available natural yarns, trial rayons, metallic strip and cellophane. He guided free-lance and house designers to issue sensitive machine woven woven interpretations of their work (plate 101, plate 111) while he also provided much of the ground work for Edinburgh Weavers - subsequently so successfully directed by Alastair Morton. Coming from a family dedicated to textiles and the manufacture of top quality design he commissioned the most talented professional designers as well as artists. Throughout the 1930s this resulted in an impressive and immensely varied output, which ranged from Ashley Havinden's graceful scrolls, soaring birds and meandering ribbons (plate 108) to the pure geometric patterns of the "Constructivist Fabrics" by Ben Nicholson and Barbara Hepworth (plates 115, 116). Birds in flight were favourite 1930s motifs and frequently used by Marion Dorn, the most successful free-lance designer of the decade. Her design, "Cyprus" (plate 107), in which lustrous mercerised cotton is set against a non-reflective ground, was one of Donald Brothers famed *Old Glamis Fabrics* which made significant contributions to the development of modern textile design.

Throughout the 1930s government-sponsored concerns – especially the Rural Industries Bureau, as well as particular craft guilds, societies and associations (the Guild of Spinners Weavers and Dyers, the Red Rose Guild and the Embroiderers Guild) – promoted the well-being of traditional crafts. Phyllis Barron and Dorothy Larcher were amongst the foremost exponents of hand block-printing with natural dyes. They printed with early French wood-blocks in addition to cutting their own designs. Aniline dyes were anathema. They skilfully devised vegetable dye recipes and perfected neglected discharge-printing methods. Bold monochrome prints on unbleached linens and cottons (plates 92, 93, 94) were their forte. During the First World War the textile industry focussed on production of goods essential to the war effort and once again in September 1939, the needs of the war became paramount. Textile factories whose output was considered non-essential to war needs were closed down, while the remaining firms (faced with labour problems and shortage of raw materials) began to manufacture necessities such as black-out material, waterproof and gasproof sheeting, parachute silk and camouflage prints. From the end of 1939 until the later 1940s, while war-time restrictions were in force, there were, not surprisingly, no outstanding textile design developments in Great Britain.

NOTES

1. *Reports on the Present Position and Tendencies of the INDUSTRIAL ARTS as indicated at the International Exhibition of Modern Decorative and Industrial Arts, Paris, 1925.* Department of Overseas Trade, 1927 .

2. Ward-Jackson, C. H., *A History of Courtaulds*, Curwen Press, 1941

3. Label on Circ.622 – 1956 (plate 38).

4. *Omega Workshops Ltd, Artist Decorators* (a catalogue of their products), London, about 1915.

5. Morton Jocelyn, *Three Generations in a Family Textile Firm*, Routledge & Kegan Paul, 1971.

6. Prospectus of the Calico Printers' Association Ltd. Incorporated under the Companies Acts 1862 to 1898

7. Calico Printers' Association Ltd. , *Fifty Years of Calico Printing*, Manchester, 1949.

8. *Vogue*, January 1, 1927 (American edition).

9. *Journal of Royal Society of Arts*, April 4, 1941.

10. *Journal of Royal Society of Arts*, January 4, 1935

PLATES

1. Stems bearing formalised roses and buds. Designed by
Mackay Hugh Baillie Scott, about 1905.
Hand block-printed cotton.
Detail, 16 x 24 in. (40.7 x 61 cm)
Circ.191B-1953.

2. Rows of small stylised peacocks. 1900-05
Hand block-printed silk dress fabric.
13½ x 26 in. (34.3 x 66 cm)
Circ.240-1966.

3. "POPPYLAND", stems bearing poppies and seed pods.
Designed and manufactured for Liberty & Co., London,
1912-13.
Duplex-printed cotton.
Detail, 13 x 14⅝ in. (33 x 37 cm)
T.324-1976.

4. "CLOVER", flowering and leafing clover stems. Designed and
manufactured for Liberty & Co., London, 1906-09.
Duplex-printed cotton.
Detail, 12⅝ x 14⅝ in. (32 x 37 cm)
T.304-1976.

5. "BEAULY", beribboned rose trees and vertical lines of roses.
Possibly designed by Jessie Marion King, and manufactured
for Liberty & Co., London, about 1910.
Duplex-printed cotton.
11⅜ x 7½ in. (29 x 19 cm)
Printed cotton samples with similar stencil-like designs appear
in a Thomas Wardle & Sons pattern book now in the
Whitworth Art Gallery, Manchester.
T.318-1976.

6. "LATHAM", stylised floral design. Designed and
manufactured for Liberty & Co., London, about 1910.
Duplex-printed cotton.
11⅜ x 7½ in. (29 x 19 cm)
T.310-1976.

7. "FIELD FLOWERS", various wild flowers. Designed and
manufactured for Liberty & Co., London, about 1910.
Duplex-printed cotton.
11⅜ x 7½ in. (29 x 19 cm)
T.317-1976.

8. "BROOKSBY", dense pattern of roses, leaves and thorny
stems. Designed and manufactured for Liberty & Co.,
London, about 1910.
Duplex-printed cotton.
11⅜ x 7½ in. (29 x 19 cm)
T.311-1976.

9. "CHATSWORTH", repeat of fruiting and flowering trees and
vines. Designed by Sidney Mawson and manufactured for
Liberty & Co., London 1909.
Printed cotton.
17⅜ x 28 in. (44 x 71 cm)
Circ.415-1966.

10. "LOWTHER", intertwined leafing and flowering stems
including honeysuckle and roses, with pairs of birds. Designed
by Sidney Mawson and manufactured for Liberty & Co.,
London, 1909.
Printed cotton.
20⅛ x 31⅛ in. (51 x 79)
Circ.416-1966.

11. Clusters of primula and leaves. Newman, Smith
& Newman, Dartford, 1911.
Printed cotton.
23 x 16 in. (58.5 x 40.7 cm)
T.81-1979.

12. Dense floral and foliate pattern. Newman, Smith
& Newman, Dartford, 1912.
Printed cotton.
18 x 14 in. (45.7 x 35.6 cm)
Circ.420-1966.

13. "WHITCHURCH", ogival framework of vines enclosing lilies and roses. Warner & Sons, Braintree, 1925.
Hand-woven rayon and metallic threads.
36 x 24 in. (91.5 x 60.9 cm)
Advertised by the firm as being 'suitable for ecclesiastical use'.
T.484-1934.

14. Large-scale pattern of ogees enclosing formalised pineapple motifs. Conceived by Frank Warner, woven by W. Watson, Warner & Sons, Braintree, December 1915.
Hand-woven silk velvet and metallic thread.
Detail, 60 x 24 in. (152 x 60.9 cm)
Pattern based on late medieval Italian velvets in the Victoria and Albert Museum.
T.163-1930.

15. Diamond trellis enclosing summer flowers with butterflies, and an owl with prey perched on an oak branch. Designed and worked by Mrs Archibald Christie, about 1914.
Embroidered panel in a wide variety of stitches including satin, stem, long and short, bullion, French knots, open work and couching in silks on a figured linen ground.
Detail of half, 21 x 34 in. (53.3 x 86.4 cm)
Circ.466-1953.

16. Ogival framework enclosing vines. Designed by Ronald Simpson (1890-1960) for Alexander Morton & Co., Carlisle, 1909.
Roller-printed cotton.
Detail, 20 x 28 in. (50.8 x 71.1 cm)
Circ.867-1967.

17. Oak leaves and meandering stems. Turnbull & Stockdale, Ltd., Ramsbottom, Lancashire, 1910.
Printed cotton.
Detail, 10 x 18 in. (25.4 x 45.8 cm)
T.80-1979.

18. Ogival framework enclosing leaves and flowers. Newman, Smith & Newman, Dartford, 1911.
Printed cotton.
22 x 14 in. (55.9 x 35.6 cm)
Circ.418-1966.

19. Intertwined leafing and flowering stems. Newman, Smith & Newman, Dartford, 1909.
Printed cotton.
17 x 10 in. (43.2 x 25.4 cm)
Circ.417-1966.

20. "CRACOW", abstract linear pattern. Designed by a member of the Omega workshops, London, manufactured by A. H. Lee & Sons, Birkenhead, 1913.
Jacquard woven, block-printed wool and linen.
Detail, 25 x 22 in. (63.5 x 55.9 cm)
T.460-1934.

21. "AMENOPHIS", abstract design of overlapped irregular planes and part ovals decorated with brush marks. Designed by a member of the Omega Workshops, London, probably the founder, Roger Fry, printed at the Maromme Printworks, Rouen, 1913.
Printed linen.
24 x 31 in. (61 x 78.5 cm)
Based on a Roger Fry oil painting "Still Life with Eggs and Books", about 1912.
Misc.2(40)-1934.

22. "MARGERY", cones with infills of brush strokes. Designed by a member of the Omega Workshops, London, printed at the Maromme Printworks, Rouen, 1913.
Printed linen.
26¹/₂ x 30 in. (67.3 x 76.2 cm)
Circ. 423-1966.

23. "WHITE", linear, striped, step pattern over colour patches. Designed by a member of the Omega Workshops, London, printed at the Maromme Printworks, Rouen, 1913.
Printed linen.
30 x 30 in. (76.2 x 76.2 cm)
Design registered in July 1914.
Registered number 109912.
T.84-1979.

24. "PAMELA", arc and angle pattern formed by bold lines and scalloped bands. Designed by a member of the Omega Workshops, London, printed at the Maromme Printworks, Rouen, 1913.
Printed linen.
19 x 31 in. (48.3 x 78.7 cm)
Circ.426-1966.

25. "MECHTILDE", rows of squares linked by vertical lines. Designed by a member of the Omega Workshops, London, possibly Frederick Etchells, printed at the Maromme Printworks, Rouen, 1913.
Printed linen.
19 x 31 in. (48.3 x 78.8 cm)
This simple design was also used for a carpet woven by The Wilton Royal Carpet Factory, near Salisbury, about 1915.
Misc.2(41)-1934.

26. "MAUD", abstract design of blocks with jagged edges and broken lines. Designed by a member of the Omega Workshops, printed at the Maromme Printworks, Rouen, 1913.
Printed linen.
32 x 30¹/₂ in. (81.3 x 77.5 cm)
Circ.425-1966.

27. Lines of crescents. Designed by Charles Rennie Mackintosh for William Foxton, London, 1918.
Printed silk.
Detail, 29 x 27 in. (73.7 x 68.6 cm)
T.43-1953.

28. Diagonal meanders of flame-like devices on an irregular mesh sub-pattern. Probably designed by Charles Rennie Mackintosh for William Foxton, London, 1918.
Printed cotton.
19 x 31 in. (48.3 x 78.7 cm)
Design registered in 1918.
T.85-1979.

29. "BLUE ROSES", geometric framework enclosing stylised roses. Designed by Percy Bilbie for F. W. Grafton & Co., Manchester, 1921.
Roller-printed cotton.
38 x 35¹/₂ in. (96.5 x 90.2 cm)
Circ.615-1964.

30. All-over chevron design. Designed by Claud Lovat Fraser for William Foxton, London, 1920.
Roller-printed cotton.
Detail, 19 x 30 in. (48.3 x 76.2 cm)
T.375-1934.

31. Trellis with large bunches of flowers and fruits.
F. W. Grafton & Co., Manchester, 1921.
Roller-printed cotton.
Detail, 44 x 34 in. (111.8 x 86.4 cm)
T.442-1934.

32. Fanciful tree trunks with decorative growths.
F. Steiner & Co., Church, Lancashire, 1920.
Roller-printed cotton.
22 x 31 in. (55.9 x 78.7 cm)
T.87-1979.

33. Floral arrangements in ovals on a flower-strewn ground.
F. W. Grafton & Co., Manchester, 1920.
Roller-printed cotton.
36 x 35 in. (91.5 x 88.9 cm)
Circ.444-1966.

34. Impressionist floral design. Designed by George Sheringham for Seftons, Belfast, 1921.
Printed silk dress fabric.
Detail, 32 x 20 in. (81.3 x 50.8 cm)
T.355-1934.

35. Clusters of stylised fruits, flowers and shell motifs. Designed by George Sheringham for Seftons, Belfast, 1922.
Printed silk.
28 x 26 in. (71.1 x 66 cm)
T.396-1934.

36. Single flowers within vertical bands, over chevron stripes. Calico Printers' Association, Manchester, 1920.
Roller-printed cotton.
Detail, 30 x 24 in. (76.2 x 61 cm)
T.86-1979.

37. Arch pattern in black and greys. Designed by F Gregory Brown for William Foxton, London, 1922.
Printed linen.
Detail, 44 x 37 in. (111.8 x 94 cm)
Exhibited at L'Exposition Internationale des Arts Décoratifs et Industriels Modernes, Paris, 1925.
T.325-1934.

38. Geometrically decorated vertical stripes. Designed by Constance Irving for William Foxton, London, 1921.
Roller-printed cotton.
Detail, 26 x 30 in. (66 x 76.2 cm)
Circ.622-1956.

39. Vertical stripes with circles. Calico Printers' Association, Manchester, 1921.
Roller-printed cotton.
24 x 34 in. (61 x 86.4 cm)
Circ.453-1956.

40. Lines of roundels. Designed by Minnie McLeish for William Foxton, London, 1921.
Roller-printed cotton
T.412-1934

41. Stems and looping tendrils with harebells. Designed by Constance Irving for William Foxton, London, 1921.
Roller-printed cotton.
36 x 31 in. (91.5 x 78.8 cm)
Circ.621-1966.

42. Decorated ovals and vertical stripes. Calico Printers' Association, Manchester, 1921.
Printed cotton voile dress fabric.
17 x 18 in. (43.2 x 45.7 cm)
T.61-1979.

43. Network of circles and bands. Calico Printers' Association, Manchester, 1921.
31 x 35 in. (78.8. x 88.9 cm)
Printed cotton.
T.88-1979.

44. Geometric framework enclosing flower heads. Calico Printers' Association, Manchester, 1919.
Roller-printed cotton.
27 x 36 in. (68.6 x 91.5 cm)
Circ.438-1966.

45. Marbled pattern of large flowers within stripes and diamonds. Calico Printers' Association, Manchester, 1921.
Roller-printed cotton.
24 x 36 in. (61 x 91.5 cm)
Circ.449-1960.

46. Printed cotton voile, F. Steiner & Co, 1920.
T.59-1975.

47. Printed woollen plush, T. F. Firth & Sons, 1926.
T.105-1979.

48. Festoons of leaves and berries with Chinese lanterns and small birds. Calico Printers' Association, Manchester, 1924.
Printed cotton.
26 1/2 x 31 in. (67.3 x 78.8 cm)
Circ.477-1966.

49. Printed cotton, Calico Printers Association, 1921.
T.91-1979

50. Crinoline ladies in formal gardens. F. W. Grafton & Co.,
Manchester, 1923.
Roller-printed cotton.
Detail, 37 x 34 in. (94 x 86.4 cm)
Circ. 443-1934

51. Large-scale, leafing and flowering stems with exotic birds.
Possibly designed by Minnie McLeish for W. Foxton Ltd.,
London 1920-25.
Roller-printed cotton.
Detail, 52 x 28 in. (132.1 x 71.1 cm)
Circ.667-1966.

52. Large cubist flowers and leaves. Possibly designed by
Minnie McLeish for W. Foxton Ltd., London, 1920-25.
Roller-printed cotton.
38 x 30 in. (96.5 x 76.2 cm)
Circ.628-1956.

53. *Contre-jour* design of vines and clusters of fruit and
flowers. The Ramsden Wood Printworks, Walsden,
Todmorden, Lancashire, 1924.
Block-printed cotton.
Detail, 43 x 24 in. (109.3 x 61 cm)
Circ.468-1966.

54. Formal gardens enclosed by stylised trees. Calico Printers'
Association, Manchester, 1924.
Roller-printed cotton.
23 x 29 in. (58.4 x 73.7 cm)
Circ.471-1966.

55. Foliate cascades and floral clusters.
Calico Printers' Association, Manchester 1921.
Roller-printed cotton.
33 x 35 in. (83.9 x 88.9 cm)
T.89-1979.

56. Conventionalised floral sprays.
Calico Printers' Association, Manchester, 1927.
Roller-printed cotton.
30 x 29½ in. (76.2 x 75 cm)
Circ.490-1966.

57. Clusters of circles crossed by barbs.
Calico Printers' Association, Manchester, 1927.
Roller-printed cotton.
38 x 31 in. (96.5 x 78.8. cm)
T.92-1979.

58. Stylised flowers, blossom and leaves.
Morton Sundour Fabrics, Carlisle, 1922-24.
Jacquard woven double-cloth, cotton, silk and cotton chenille.
34 x 25 in. (86.4 x 63.5 cm)
Exhibited at L'Exposition Internationale des Arts Décoratifs
et Industriels Modernes, Paris, 1925.
Circ.884-1967.

59. Long-tailed birds and blossom stems within borders.
Designed and executed by Miss Winifred Kennedy Scott,
Glasgow, 1924-26.
Part of a shawl, wax resist dyed silk.
Detail of half, 40 x 30 in. (101.5 x 76.3 cm)
T.114-1975.

60. Interlocking segmented circles. Arthur Sanderson
& Sons, Uxbridge, 1930.
Roller-printed cotton.
29 x 30 in. (73.7 x 76.2 cm)
Circ.505-1966.

61 & 62. Rows of stylised bamboo. W. Foxton Ltd.,
London 1929.
Roller-printed cotton (two colourways).
Each, 14 x 31 in. (35.6 x 78.8 cm)
Circ.672-1966, T.93-1979.

63. Cubist floral pattern. Designed by Frank Ormrod for
Turnbull & Stockdale, Ramsbottom, Lancashire, 1929.
Roller-printed cotton.
Detail, 39 x 30 in. (99.1 x 76.2 cm)
T.386-1934.

64. Bold design of pair of angels and a central archway
enclosing a chalice. Designed by Duncan Grant, cut by
Vanessa Bell, worked by Many Hogarth, Mrs Antrobus and
Miss Elwes, 1927.
Embroidered ecclesiastical banner. Appliqué of various fabrics
embroidered mainly in wools in long and short, satin, fish-
bone, oriental and couching stitches, with glass beads.
72 x 36 in. (182.8 x 91.5 cm)
Given to the Museum in memory of Mary Hogarth
"who did so much to encourage and improve needlework
in Great Britain".
T.52-1935.

65. "ALICE IN WONDERLAND", roller-printed cotton, C. F. A.
Voysey, Morton Sundour Fabrics, about 1930.
C.856-1967.

66. Abstract stepped pattern incorporating radiating motifs.
Calico Printers' Association, Manchester, 1929.
Warp-printed cotton.
22 x 25 in. (55.9 x 63.5 cm)
T.94-1979.

67. All-over design of fan shapes.
Franklin & Franklin, Manchester, 1934.
Warp-printed cotton.
Detail, 26 x 35 in. (66 x 88.9 cm)
Circ.542-1966.

68. Vertical bands and chevron stripes.
Arthur Sanderson & Sons, Uxbridge, 1930.
Warp-printed cotton.
35 x 24 in. (88.9 x 61 cm)
Circ. 507-1966.

69. Pairs of horsemen and trees.
Designed by F. Gregory Brown for W. Foxton Ltd.,
London, 1931.
Roller-printed linen.
Detail, 30 x 20 in. (76.2 x 50.8 cm)
T.307-1934.

70. Interlocking, Cubist abstract motifs.
Designed by F. Gregory Brown for W. Foxton Ltd,
London, 1932.
Roller-printed linen.
13 x 15 in. (33 x 38.1 cm)
T.99-1979.

71. "DIANA", figure of Diana with hound, bird and flowers.
Designed and worked by Rebecca Crompton, 1930.
Embroidered panel. White organdie over green hessian with
appliqué of white cotton, linen and metallic braid,
embroidered in white cotton mainly in chain stitch.
17^1/$_2$ x 15^1/$_4$ in. (44.5 x 38.7 cm)
T.511-1934.

72. Geometric, abstract pattern.
Designed by F. Gregory Brown for W. Foxton Ltd.,
London, 1931.
Roller-printed linen.
13 x 15 in. (33 x 38.1 cm)
Circ.523-1966.

73. Bold fruit and flower design.
Arthur Sanderson & Sons, Uxbridge, 1930.
Roller-printed linen.
31 x 31 in. (78.8 x 78.8 cm)
Circ.503-1966.

74. Delphinium sprays.
Arthur Sanderson & Sons, Uxbridge, 1930.
Roller-printed linen.
34 x 31 in. (86.4 x 78.8 cm)
T.97-1979.

75. Rows of crocuses.
Arthur Sanderson & Sons, Uxbridge, 1932.
Roller-printed cotton.
23 x 31 in. (58.4 x 78.8. cm)
T.98-1979.

76. Irregular rows of crocuses.
Arthur Sanderson & Sons, Uxbridge, 1932.
Roller-printed cotton.
21 x 31 in. (53.3 x 78.8 cm)
Circ.678-1966.

77. Large-scale pattern of tulips.
Arthur Sanderson & Sons, Uxbridge, 1930.
Roller-printed cotton.
23 x 31 in. (58.5 x 78.8 cm)
Circ.515-1966.

78. Bold, painterly pattern of tulips and leaves.
Arthur Sanderson & Sons, Uxbridge, 1929.
Roller-printed cotton.
22 x 30 in. (55.9 x 76.3 cm)
Circ.574-1966.

79. Stylised flowers and trees.
Crysede Ltd., St Ives, Cornwall, 1930.
Hand block-printed silk dress fabric.
23 x 19 in. (58.4 x 48.2 cm)
T.68-1979.

80. Framework enclosing groups of monkeys beneath trees.
Crysede Ltd., St Ives, Cornwall, 1930.
Hand block-printed silk dress fabric.
28 x 19 in. (71.1 x 48.3 cm)
T.66-1979.

81. Small islands with palms surrounded by formalised waves.
Crysede Ltd., St Ives, Cornwall, 1930.
Hand block-printed silk dress fabric.
25 x 19 in. (63.5 x 48.3 cm)
T.65-1979.

82. Tree clumps. Crysede Ltd., St Ives, Cornwall, 1930.
Hand block-printed silk dress fabric.
30 x 19 in. (76.2 x 48.3 cm)
T.67-1979.

83. Flowing all-over pattern of slender leaves and flowers.
Calico Printers' Association, Manchester, 1933.
Printed cotton voile dress fabric.
22 x 34 in. (55.9 x 86.4 cm)
T.74-1979.

84. Simplified flower heads crossed by slender leaves.
Calico Printers' Association, Manchester, 1933.
Printed cotton voile dress fabric.
22 x 34 in. (55.9 x 86.4 cm)
T.72-1979.

85. Flowers on a leafy ground. Calico Printers' Association,
Manchester, 1933.
Printed cotton voile dress fabric.
23 x 35 in. (58.4 x 88.9 cm)
T.73-1979.

86. Blossom clusters. Calico Printers' Association,
Manchester, 1937.
Printed cotton crêpe dress fabric.
18 x 35 in. (45.7 x 88.9 cm)
T.79-1979.

87. Pattern of anemones. Calico Printers' Association,
Manchester, 1935.
Printed cotton crêpe dress fabric.
22 x 34 in. (55.9 x 86.4 cm)
T.78-1979.

88. Spot repeat of seeds. Calico Printers' Association,
Manchester, 1934.
Printed cotton voile dress fabric.
18 x 32 in. (45.7 x 81 cm)
T.75-1979.

89. Small-scale mixed flower pattern. Liberty & Co.,
London, 1938.
Printed cotton crêpe dress fabric ('Runis' crêpe).
12¹/₂ x 11 in. (31.8 x 28 cm)
T.113-1979.

90. Small-scale mixed flower pattern. Liberty & Co.,
London, 1938
Printed cotton crêpe dress fabric ('Runis' crêpe).
15 x 13 in. (38.2 x 33 cm)
T.114-1979.

91. "POPPY AND DAISY", bordered design of small poppies,
daisies and other field flowers. Liberty & Co., London, 1929-30.
Hand block-printed silk handkerchief.
17 x 18 in. (43.2 x 45.8 cm)
T.283-1976.

92. "POINTED PIP", vertical bands with serrated edges and pips.
Designed and printed by Phyllis Barron and Dorothy Larcher,
Painswick, Gloucestershire, 1930s.
Hand block-printed linen.
Detail, 28 x 36 in. (71.1 x 91.4 cm)
Circ.301-1938.

93. "HAZLITT", vertical broken bands with diagonal stripes
in black on an unbleached ground. Designed and printed
by Phyllis Barron and Dorothy Larcher, Painswick,
Gloucestershire, 1930s.
Hand block-printed linen.
Detail, 37 x 36 in. (94 x 91.4 cm)
Misc.2(42)-1934.

94. "SMALL FEATHER", feathers and spots. Designed
and printed by Dorothy Larcher, Painswick,
Gloucestershire, 1930s.
Hand block-printed (discharged indigo) linen.
Detail, 28 x 36 in. (71.1 x 91.4 cm)
Misc.2(52)-1934.

95. Cloud images. Designed by Duncan Grant for
Allan Walton Textiles, London 1932-33.
Screen-printed cotton and rayon.
30 x 42 in. (76.2 x 106.7 cm)
T.301-1934.

96. "LITTLE URN", urns containing floral arrangements.
Designed by Duncan Grant for Allan Walton Textiles,
London, 1932-33.
Screen-printed cotton and rayon.
25 x 29 in. (63.5 x 73.7 cm)
T.302-1934.

97. Repeat of large leaves and flowers. Designed by
Duncan Grant for Allan Walton Textiles, London, 1936.
Screen-printed cotton velvet.
50 x 30 in. (127 x 76.2 cm)
Commissioned by the Cunard White Star Steamship Company
for the lounge of the liner 'Queen Mary', but at the last
moment the scheme was rejected.
Circ.410-1954.

98. Repeat of a lower vase lit by rays from a table lamp.
Designed by Vanessa Bell for Allan Walton Textiles, London,
1934-36.
Screen-printed cotton and rayon.
Detail, 44 x 36 in. (111.8 x 91.5 cm)
Circ.88-1937.

99. "DAPHNE AND APOLLO", figurative design with diagonal
emphasis – Daphne scatters flowers to a pursuing Apollo,
in two blues, pink, yellow, terra-cotta, beige and brown on
cream. Designed by Duncan Grant for Allan Walton Textiles,
London, 1932-33.
Screen-printed cotton and rayon.
Detail, 60 x 38 in. (152.5 x 96.5 cm)
Circ. 357-1938.

100. "FUGUE", abstract pattern incorporating circles.
Designed by Paul Nash for The Old Bleach Linen Company,
Randalstown, 1936.
Screen-printed linen with textured weave.
34¹/₂ x 22 in. (87.6 x 55.9 cm)
Circ.462-1962.

101. "MENDIP", meandering horizontal bands and stripes.
Designed by Charles Grant for Warner & Sons, Braintree,
Essex, 1934.
Jacquard woven cotton.
18 x 25 in. (45.8 x 63.5 cm)
Circ.187A-1935.

102. Large circles decorated with squares, linked by horizontal
whiplashes. Designed by Frederick Oliver Roy Plaistow for
Courtaulds Ltd., Halstead, Essex, about 1931.
Jacquard woven cotton and rayon.
23¹/₂ x 25 in. (59.7 x 63.5 cm)
Exhibited Exposition Internationale des Arts et Techniques
dans la Vie Moderne, Paris 1937.
Circ.38-1938.

103. Repeat of two confronted, dancing girls linked
by ribbons swirling from their hands, in black and dull orange
printers' inks on natural. Designed and printed by Frank
Dobson, London, 1938-39.
Hand block (lino) printed linen.
Detail, 50 x 44 in. (127 x 111.8 cm)
Circ.9-1939.

104. Large abstract buds linked by diagonal line on an all-over
arc pattern of brush marks. Designed by Frank Dobson for
Allan Walton Textiles, London, about 1933.
Screen-printed cotton and rayon.
Detail, 38 x 28 in. (96.5 x 71.1 cm)
Circ. 353-1938.

105. Diagonal stripes and meandering bands. Designed by
H. J. Bull for Allan Walton Textiles, London, 1932.
Screen-printed cotton and rayon.
Detail, 38 x 28 in. (96.5 x 71.1 cm)
T.305-1934.

106. Fret pattern. Designed by T. Bradley for Allan Walton
Textiles, London, 1935-36
Screen-printed cotton and rayon.
Detail, 30 x 48 in. (76.2 x 121.9 cm)
Circ.361-1938.

107. "CYPRUS", ionic pillars crossed by pairs of birds in flight
bearing ivy trails. Designed by Marion Dorn for Donald
Brothers Ltd., Dundee, 1936.
Jacquard woven cotton.
Detail, 31 x 22 in. (78.9 x 55.9 cm)
Circ.521-1954.

108. "UCCELLO", vertical riband stripes crossed by diagonal
rows of doves in flight and olive branches. Designed by Ashley
Havinden for Edinburgh Weavers, Carlisle, 1937-38.
Jacquard woven cotton.
Detail, 30 x 20 in. (76.2 x 50.8 cm)
Circ.463-1939.

109. "LANGTON", two vertical columns of spiralling ribbons
intertwined with leafing stems in two greens, salmon pink
and beige on pink.
Designed by Marion Dorn for Donald Brothers, Dundee, 1938.
Screen-printed linen and rayon.
Detail, 60 x 48 in. (152.5 x 121.9 cm)
Circ.291-1938.

110. "AIRCRAFT", repeat of pairs of stylised birds in flight, in
navy, green, yellow, turquoise on natural. Designed by Marion
Dorn for the Old Bleach Linen Company, Randalstown, 1938.
Screen-printed linen and rayon.
Detail, 48 x 36 in. (121.9 x 91.5 cm)
Used in the lounge of the liner 'Orcades'.
Circ.241-1939.

111. Fret pattern in cream tones. Probably designed by
Marion Dorn for Warner & Sons, Braintree, about 1935.
Jacquard woven cotton upholstery velvet, pattern formed by
cut and uncut pile on voided ground.
36 x 24¹/₂ in. (91.5 x 62.3 cm)
Circ.525-1954.

112. Various overlapped rectangles, L shapes and stripes. Designed by Edward McKnight Kauffer for The Wilton Royal Carpet Factory, near Salisbury, 1929.
Rug, hand-knotted woollen pile on a jute warp.
44³/₄ x 73 in. (113.7 x 185.5 cm)
T.440-1971.

113. Central riband spiral crossed by ears of bearded wheat. Designed by Marion Dorn for The Wilton Royal Carpet Factory, near Salisbury, about 1936.
Rug, hand-knotted woollen pile on a jute warp.
83 x 43 in. (210.8 x 109.3 cm)
Circ.481-1974.

114. Abstract design of a loose trefoil and three parallel, non-continuous stripes. Designed by Ashley Havinden, probably for Edinburgh Weavers, Carlisle, about 1937.
Carpet, hand-knotted woollen pile on a jute warp.
96 x 70 in. (243.8 x 177.8 cm)
T.380-1976.

115. "HORIZONTAL", geometric design based on L shapes and rectangles. Designed by Ben Nicholson for Edinburgh Weavers, Carlisle, 1937.
Jacquard woven cotton and rayon.
Detail, 50 x 20 in. (127 x 50.8 cm)
A textile from the range of 'Constructivist Fabrics' issued by the firm in Autumn 1937.
Circ.172-1938.

116. "THREE CIRCLES", horizontal bands decorated with circles, and vertical bands with various stripes, in lilac, pink, scarlet and black on white. Designed by Ben Nicholson for Edinburgh Weavers, Carlisle, 1937.
Screen-printed linen and rayon.
Detail, 42 x 30 in. (106.7 x 76.2 cm)
A textile from the range of 'Constructivist Fabrics' issued by the firm in Autumn, 1937.
Circ.470-1939.

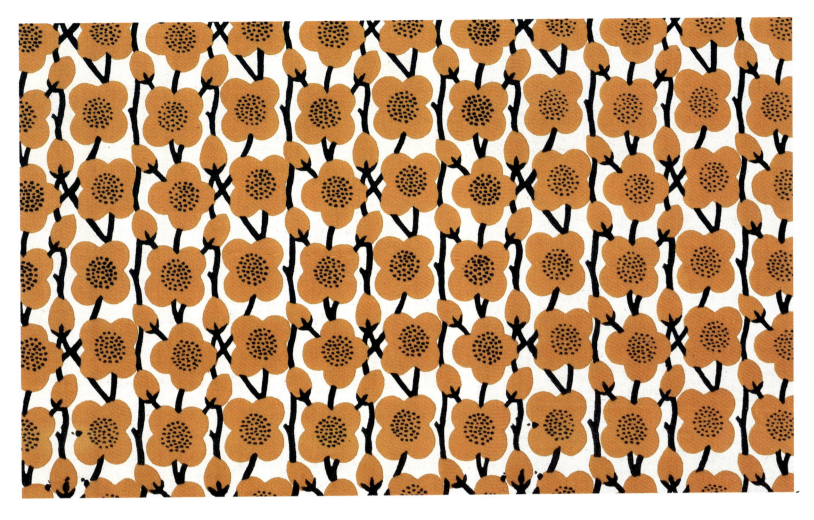

1: Block-printed cotton. M. H. Baillie-Scott, about 1905. T.135-1972
2: Block-printed silk, 1900-05. Circ.240-1966

30

3: "POPPYLAND", duplex-printed cotton. Liberty & Co., 1912-13. T.324-1976
4: "CLOVER", duplex-printed cotton. Liberty & Co., 1906-9. T.304-1976

5: "BEAULY", duplex-printed cotton. Liberty & Co., about 1910. T.318-1976. Detail
6: "LATHAM", duplex-printed cotton. Liberty & Co., about 1910.
T.310-1976. Detail

5

6

7

8

7: "FIELD FLOWERS", duplex-printed cotton. Liberty & Co., about 1910.
T.317-1976. Detail
8: "BROOKSBY", duplex-printed cotton. Liberty & Co., about 1910. T.311-1976. Detail

32

9

10

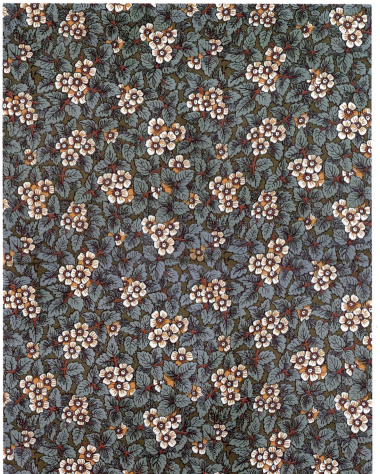

11

12

11: Printed cotton. Newman, Smith & Newman, 1911. T.81-1979. Detail
12: Printed cotton. Newman, Smith & Newman, 1912. Circ.420-1966. Detail

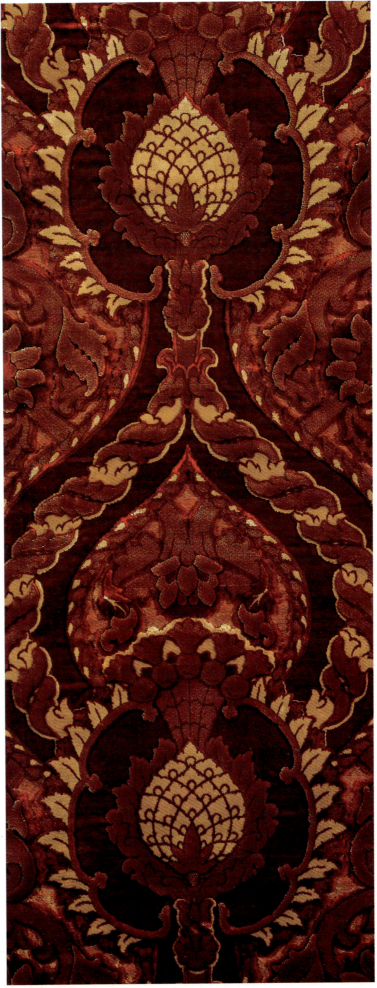

13: "WHITCHURCH", woven rayon and metallic threads. Warner & Sons, 1925. T.484-1934. Detail
14: Hand-woven silk velvet. Warner & Sons, 1915. T.163-1930. Detail

15: Embroidered panel. Mrs Archibald Christie, about 1914.
Circ.466-1953. Detail

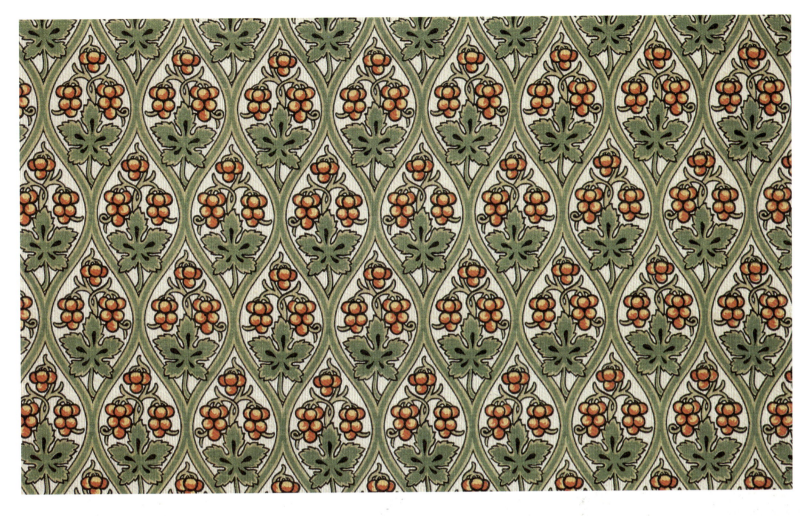

16: Roller-printed cotton. Ronald Simpson, Alexander Morton & Co., 1909.
Circ.867-1967
17: Printed cotton. Turnbull & Stockdale Ltd., 1910. T.80-1979

36

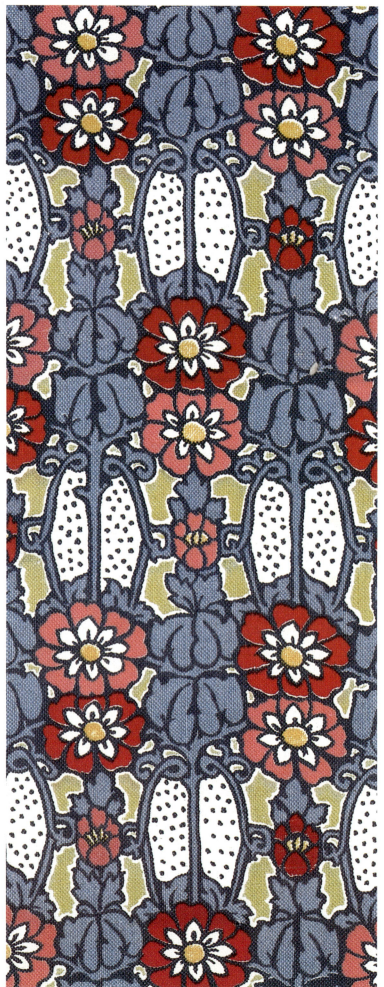

18: Printed cotton. Newman, Smith & Newman, 1911. Circ.418-1966
19: Printed cotton. Newman, Smith & Newman, 1909. Circ.417-1966

21: "Amenophis", printed linen. Omega Workshops, 1913.
Misc.2[40]-1934. Detail
22: "Margery", printed linen. Omega Workshops, 1913. Circ.423-1966. Detail

38

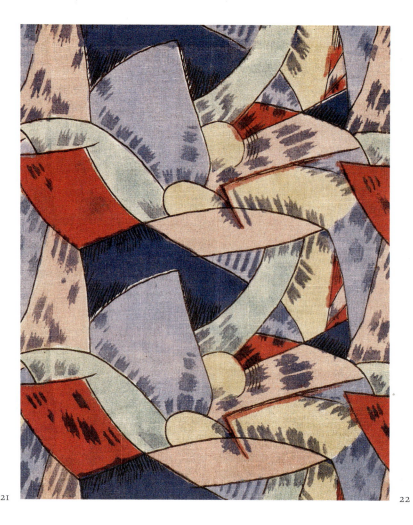

21

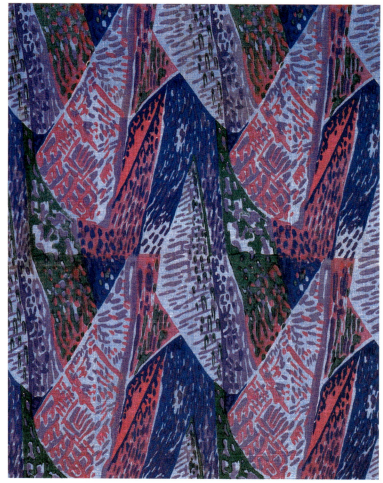

22

23

24

23: "White", printed linen. Omega Workshops, 1913. T.84-1979. Detail
24: "Pamela", printed linen. Omega Workshops, 1913. Circ.426-1966. Detail

25: "MECHTILDE", printed linen. Omega Workshops, 1913. Misc.[41]-1934. Detail
26: "MAUD", printed linen. Omega Workshops, 1913. Circ.425-1966. Detail

40

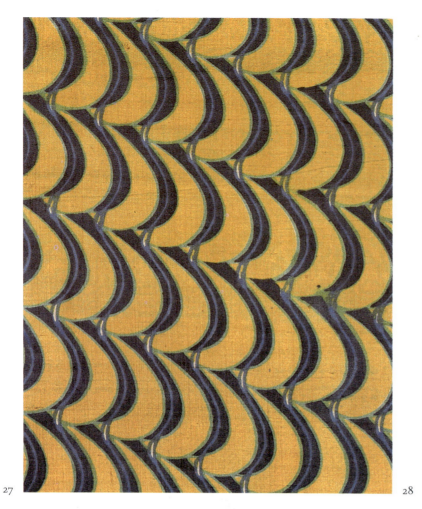

27

28

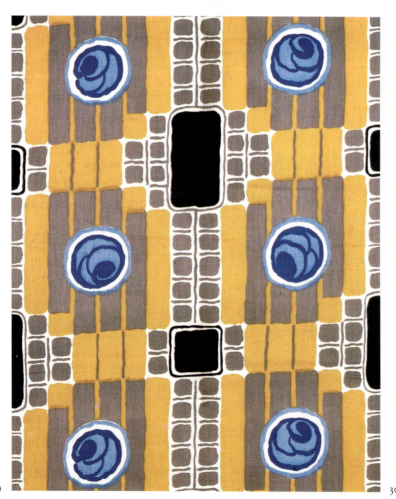

29

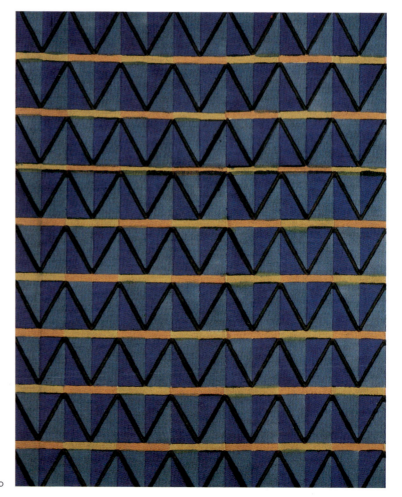

30

29: "BLUE ROSES", roller-printed cotton. Percy Bilbie, F. W. Grafton & Co., 1921.
Circ.615-1964. Detail
30: Roller-printed cotton. Claud Lovat Fraser, William Foxton, 1920. T.375-1934. Detail

31: Roller-printed cotton. F. W. Grafton & Co., 1921. T.442-1934. Detail
32: Roller-printed cotton. F. W. Grafton & Co., 1920. T.87-1979. Detail
33: Roller-printed cotton. F. W. Grafton & Co., 1920. Circ.444-1966. Detail

42

34: Printed silk dress fabric. George Sheringham for Seftons, 1921.
T.355-1934
35: Printed silk. George Sheringham for Seftons, 1922. T.396-1934

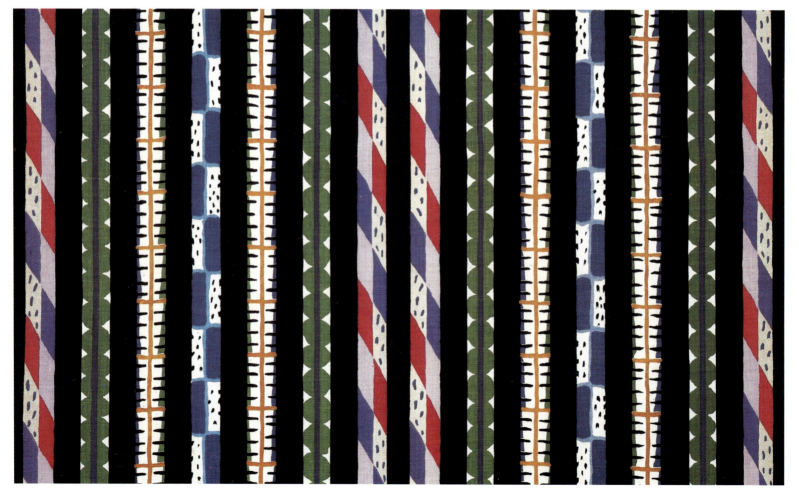

37: Printed linen. William Foxton, London, 1922. T325-1934
38: Roller-printed cotton. Constance Irving, William Foxton, 1921.
Circ.622-1956

39: Roller-printed cotton. Calico Printers' Association, 1921. Circ.453-1956. Detail
40: Roller-printed cotton. Minnie McLeish, William Foxton, London, 1921.
T.412-1934. Detail

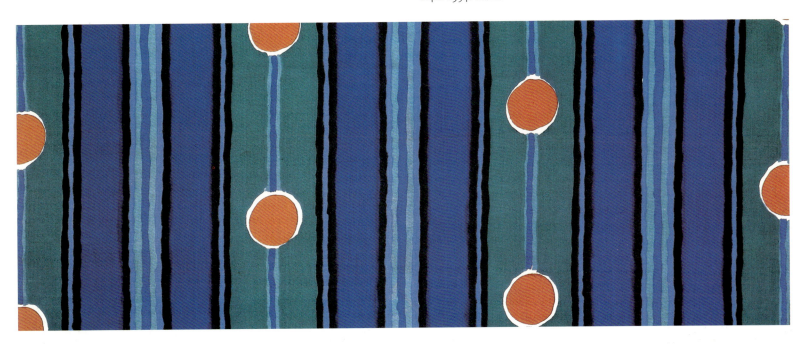

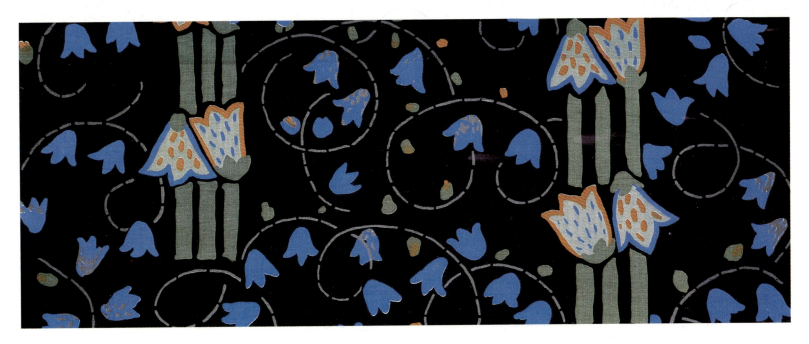

41: Roller-printed cotton. Constance Irving, William Foxton, 1921.
Circ.621-1956. Detail

46

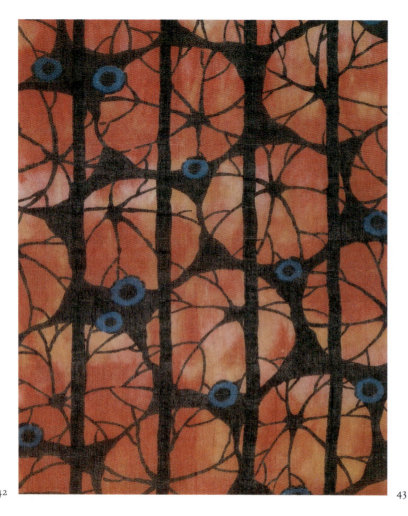

42

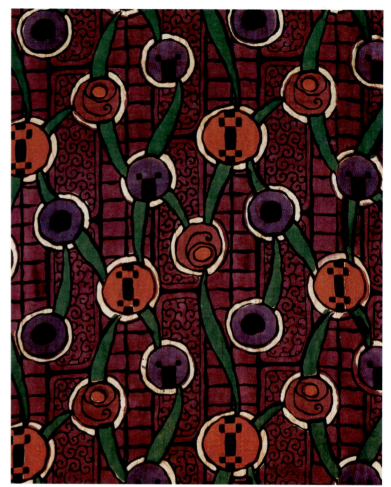

43

44

45

44: Roller-printed cottonl. Calico Printers' Association, 1919. Circ.438-1966. Detail
45: Roller-printed cotton. Calico Printers' Association, 1921. Circ.449-1966. Detail

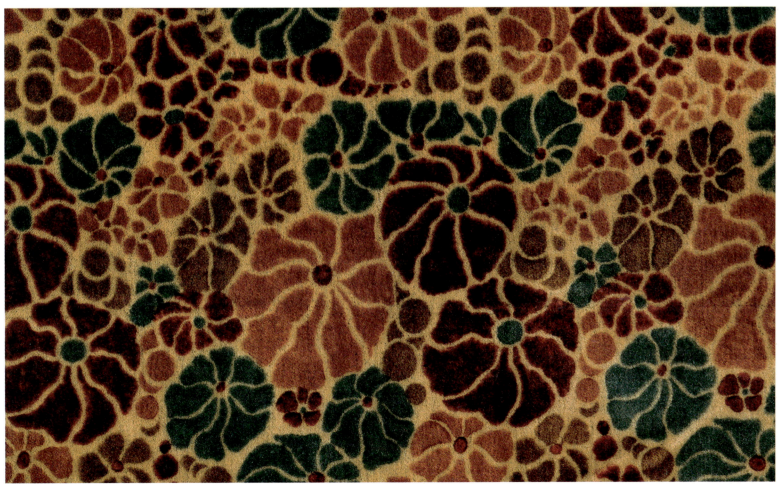

46: Printed cotton voile, F. Steiner & Co., 1920. T.59-1975.
47: Printed woollen plush, T. F. Firth & Sons, 1926. T.105-1979

48

48: Printed cotton. Calico Printers' Association, 1924. Circ.477-1966. Detail
49: Printed cotton. Calico Printers' Association, 1921. T.91-1979. Detail

50: Roller-printed cotton. F. W. Grafton & Co., 1923. Circ.443-1934

50

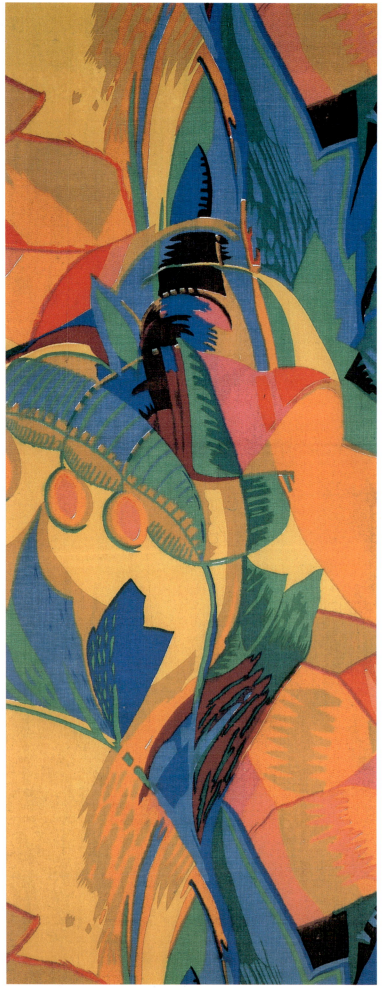

54: Roller-printed cotton. Calico Printers' Association, 1924.
Circ.471-1966. Detail
55: Roller-printed cotton. Calico Printers' Association, 1921. T.89-1979. Detail

52

56: Roller-printed cotton. Calico Printers' Association, 1927.
Circ.490-1966. Detail
57: Roller-printed cotton. Calico Printers' Association, 1927. T.92-1979. Detail

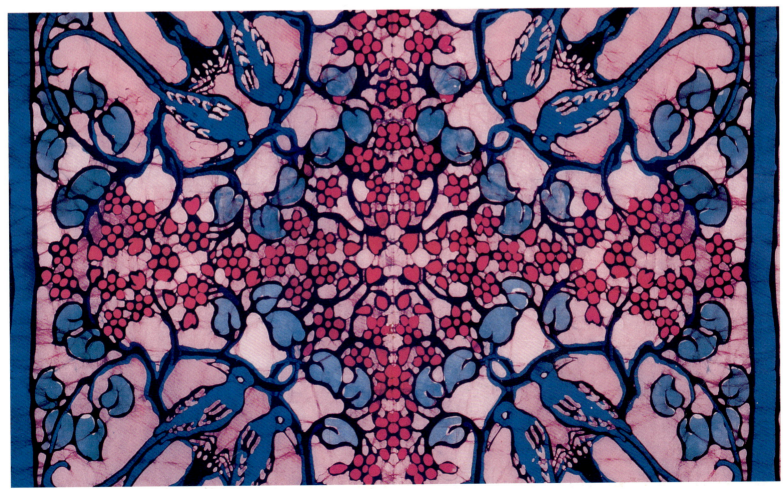

58: Jacquard woven double-cloth. Morton Sundour Fabrics, 1922-4.
Circ.884-1967. Detail
59: Shawl, silk batik. Miss Winifred Kennedy Scott, 1924-6. T.114-1975. Detail

55

61 & 62: Roller-printed cotton (two colourways). W. Foxton Ltd., 1928.
Circ.672-1966; T.93-1979

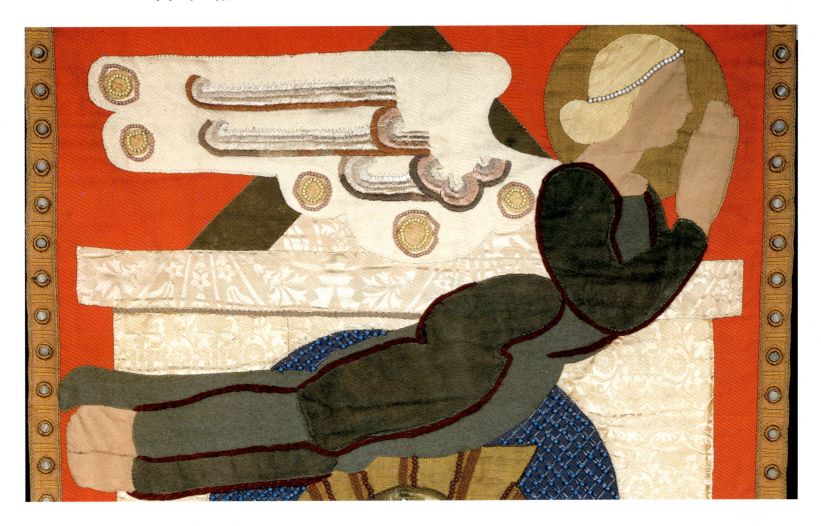

64: Embroidered ecclesiastical banner. Duncan Grant, 1927. T.52-1935. Detail
65: "ALICE IN WONDERLAND", roller-printed cotton. Morton Sundour Fabrics,
about 1930. Circ.856-1967. Detail

58

66: Warp-printed cotton. Calico Printers' Association, 1929. T.94-1979
67: Warp-printed cotton. Arthur Sanderson & Sons, 1930. Circ.542-1966

68: Warp-printed cotton. Arthur Sanderson & Sons, 1930. Circ.507-1906

69: Roller-printed linen. F. Gregory Brown for W. Foxton Ltd., 1931. T.307-1934. Detail
70: Roller-printed linen. F. Gregory Brown for W. Foxton Ltd., 1932. T.99-1979. Detail

73: Roller-printed cotton. Arthur Sanderson & Sons, 1930. Circ.503-1966. Detail

60

69

70

71

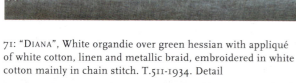

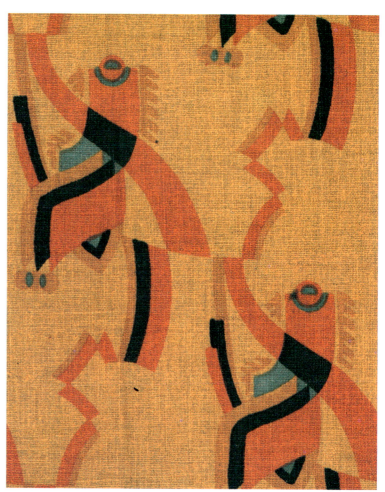

72

71: "Diana", White organdie over green hessian with appliqué of white cotton, linen and metallic braid, embroidered in white cotton mainly in chain stitch. T.511-1934. Detail

72: Roller-printed linen. F. Gregory Brown for W. Foxton Ltd., 1931. Circ.523-1966. Detail

74: Roller-printed linen. Arthur Sanderson
& Sons, 1930. T.97-1979. Detail

75: Roller-printed cotton. Arthur Sanderson & Sons, 1932. T.98-1979. Detail
76: Roller-printed cotton. Arthur Sanderson & Sons, 1932. T.678-1966. Detail

63

75

76

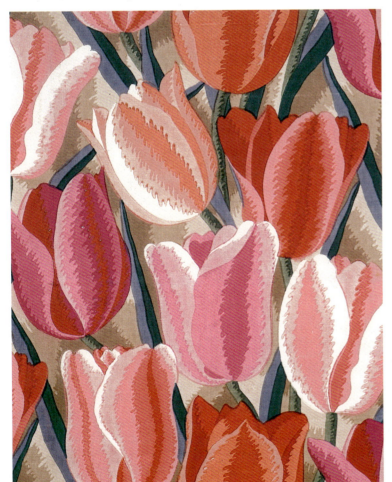

77

78

77: Roller-printed cotton. Arthur Sanderson & Sons, 1930. Circ.515-1966. Detail
78: Roller-printed cotton. Arthur Sanderson & Sons, 1929. Circ.574-1916. Detail

64

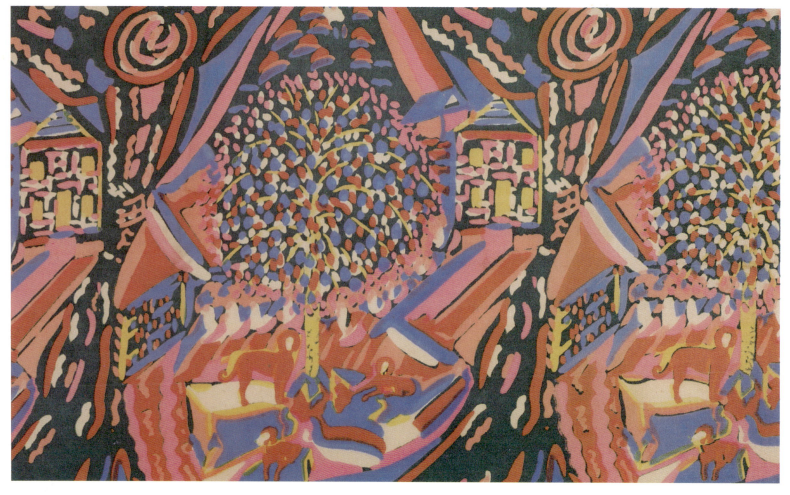

79: Block-printed silk. Crysede Ltd., 1930. T.68-1979. Detail
80: Block-printed silk. Crysede Ltd., 1930. T.66-1979. Detail

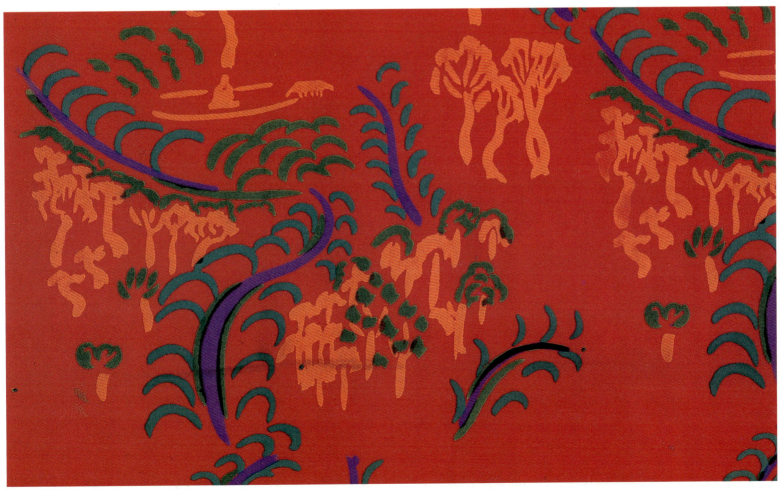

81: Block-printed silk. Crysede Ltd., 1930. T.65-1979. Detail
82: Block-printed silk. Crysede Ltd., 1930. T.67-1979. Detail

83: Printed cotton and rayon. Calico Printers' Association, 1933.
T.74-1979. Detail
84: Printed cotton voile. Calico Printers' Association, 1933. T.72-1979. Detail

66

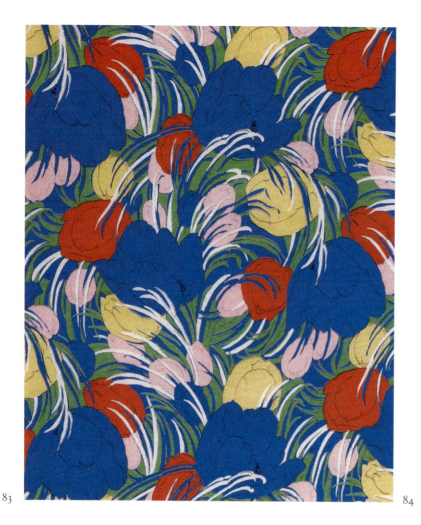

83

84

85

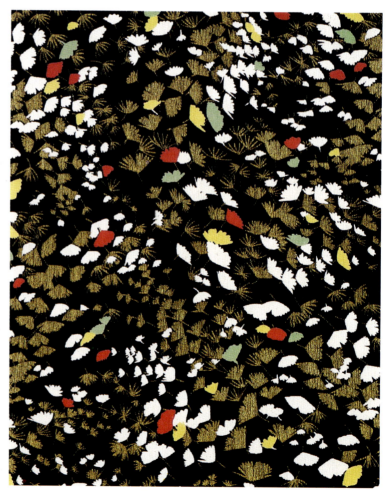

86

85: Printed cotton voile. Calico Printers' Association, 1933. T.73-1979. Detail
86: Printed cotton crêpe. Calico Printers' Association, 1937. T.79-1979. Detail

87: Printed cotton crêpe. Calico Printers' Association, 1935. T.78-1979
88: Printed cotton crêpe. Calico Printers' Association, 1934. T.75-1979

89: Printed cotton crêpe. Liberty & Co., 1938. T.113-1979. Detail
90: Printed cotton crêpe. Liberty & Co., 1938. T.114-1979. Detail

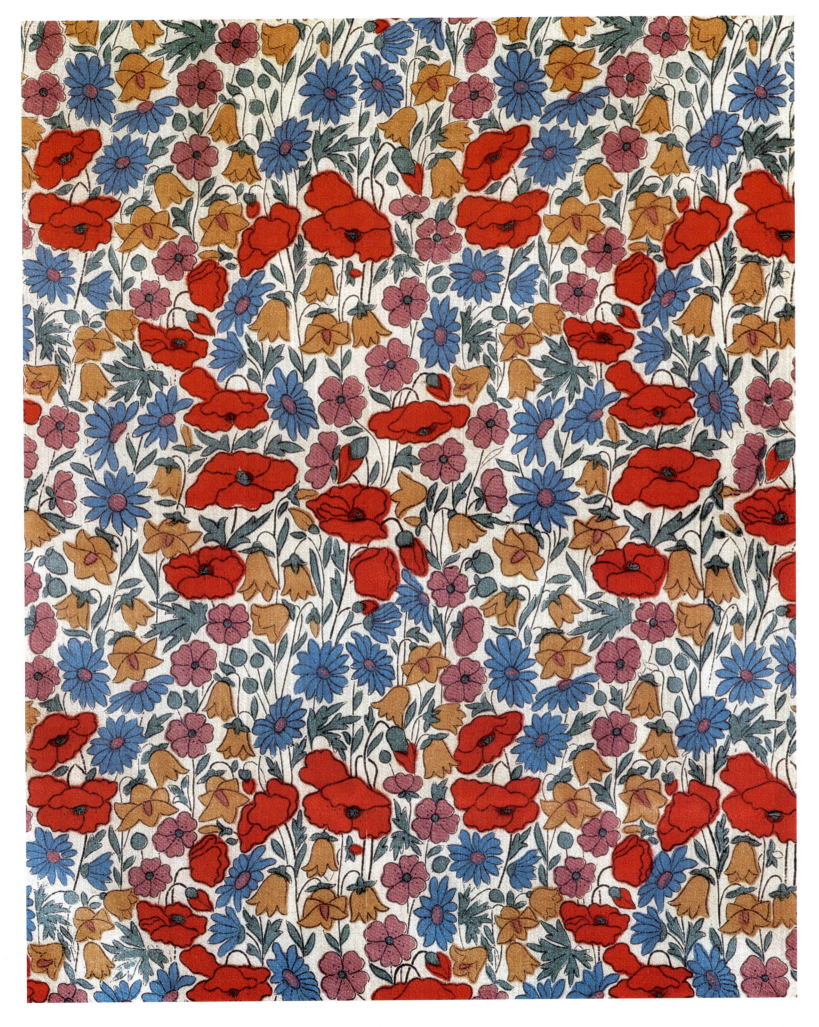

91: "Poppy and Daisy", block-printed silk. Liberty & Co., 1929-30. T.283-1976

70

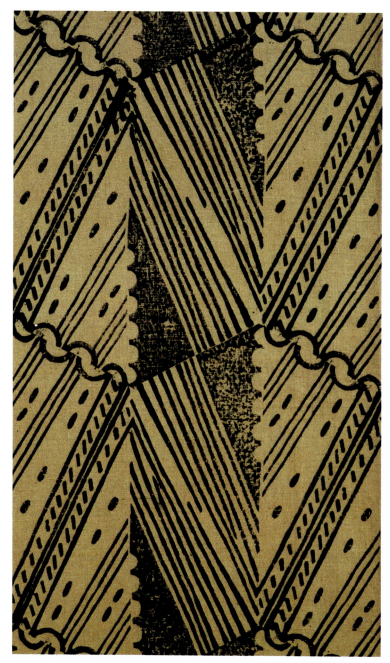

93: "HAZLITT", hand block-printed linen. Phyllis Barron and Dorothy Larcher,
1930s. Misc. 2(42)-1934. Detail

94: "SMALL FEATHER", block-printed linen. Dorothy Larcher, 1930s.
Misc.2[52]-1934. Detail

96: Screen-printed cotton and rayon. Duncan Grant, Allan
Walton Textiles, 1932-3. T.302-1934

97: Screen-printed cotton velvet. Duncan Grant, Allan Walton Textiles, 1936. Circ. 410-1954

98: Screen-printed cotton and rayon. Vanessa Bell, Allan Walton Textiles, 1934-6. Circ.88-1937. Detail

99: "DAPHNE AND APOLLO", Screen-printed cotton and rayon. Allan Walton Textiles, London, 1932-33. Circ.357-1938. Detail

100: "FUGUE", screen-printed linen. Paul Nash, The Old
Bleach Linen Company, 1936. Circ.462-1962

101: "MENDIP", jacquard woven cotton. Charles Grant, Warner
and Sons, 1934. Circ.187A-1935. Detail

75

102: Jacquard woven cotton and rayon. F. O. R. Plaistow,
Courtaulds Ltd., c.1931. Circ.38-1938. Detail

76

103: Hand block (lino) printed linen. Frank Dobson,
London, 1938-39. Circ.9-1939. Detail

78

106: Screen-printed cotton and rayon. T. Bradley, Allan
Walton Textiles, 1935-36. Circ. 361-1938. Detail

108: "Uccello", jacquard woven cotton. Designed by Ashley Havinden for
Edinburgh Weavers, Carlisle, 1937-8. Circ.463-1939. Detail

109: "LANGTON", Screen-printed linen and rayon. Donald
Brothers, Dundee, 1938. Circ.291-1938. Detail

110: "Aircraft", screen printed linen and rayon. Old Bleach
Linen Company, Randalstown, 1938. Circ.241-1939

111: Jacquard woven cotton upholstery velvet, pattern formed by cut and
uncut pile on voided ground. Warner & Sons, Braintree, about 1935.
Circ.525-1954. Detail

82

112: Rug. Marion Dorn, The Wilton Royal Carpet Factory,
about 1936. Circ.481-1974

113: Rug. E. McKnight Kauffer, The Royal Wilton
Carpet Factory, 1929. T.440-1971

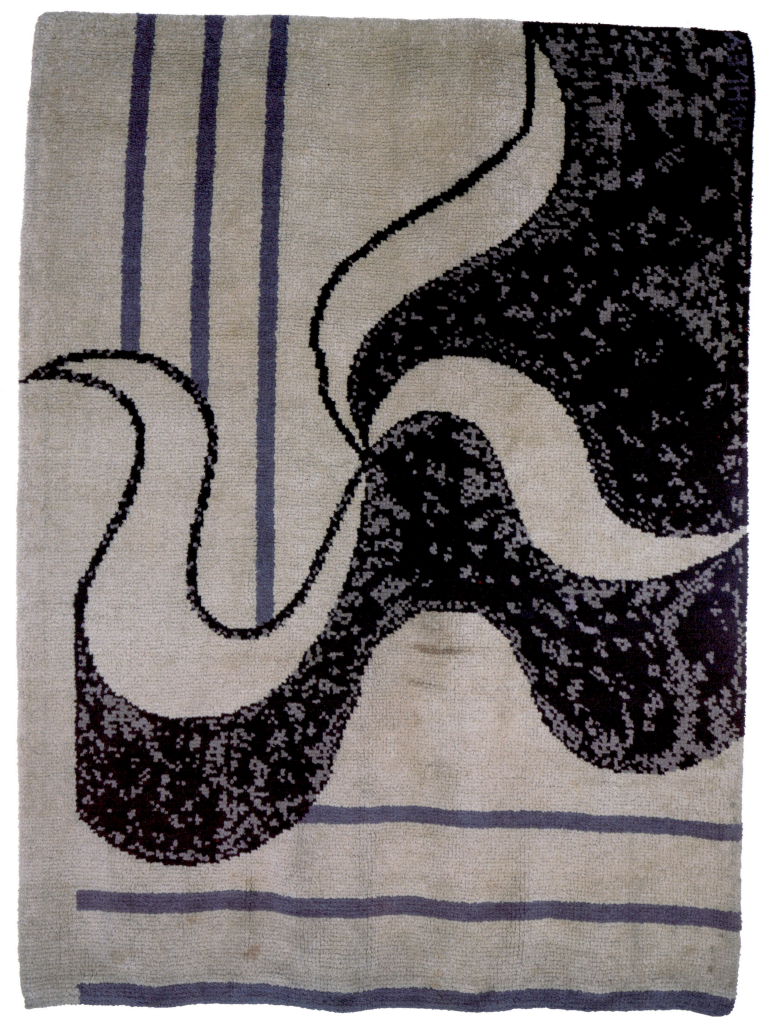

84

114: Carpet. Ashley Havinden, probably Edinburgh Weavers,
about 1937. T.380-1976

115: "Horizontal", jacquard woven cotton and rayon. Ben Nicholson,
Edinburgh Weavers, 1937. Circ. 172-1938

116: "THREE CIRCLES", screen-printed linen and rayon.
Edinburgh Weavers, Carlisle, 1937. Circ.470-1939

GLOSSARY

APPLIQUE The application (usually by means of embroidery) of shaped pieces of fabric to a ground material to create a design. In the late 19th and early 20th centuries the technique was used in a bold manner especially by embroideresses of the Glasgow School and later by Rebecca Crompton and others.

BATIK Hand technique involving the application of wax to protect the pattern areas while the textile is submerged in the dye bath. After removing the wax the process can be repeated to achieve the required number of colours. Characterised by all over fine veining where the wax has cracked and permitted the dye to penetrate. Mass production involves roller-printing the wax on to the fabric from heated rollers prior to dyeing. The hand craft became popular in European artistic centres in the 1920s.

BLOCK-PRINTING One of the oldest methods of printing. Wooden blocks have the pattern cut in relief and each colour in the pattern has a separate block. The colour is transmitted from the block face to the cloth by hitting the back of the block with the handle end of a mallet. It is a skilled, costly and laborious process and in the 20th century has been superseded by mechanised roller and screen-printing.

CHENILLE YARN A tufted weft yarn (in use from the late 17th century onwards) of cotton, silk or wool (and in the later 20th century, man-made fibres), caterpillar-like in appearance. Fabric woven with such yarns is a chenille fabric. Chenilles were popular furnishings throughout the later 19th century and until the 1930s.

CHINOISERIE The European view of Chinese decoration inspired by many disparate objects which were often not Chinese. The style of chinoiserie changed with the different aesthetic movements, but it was essentially an excuse for fanciful decoration.

CREPE Usually a dress weight fabric with textured surface achieved in various ways – use of hard-twisted yarns, application of heat or chemicals, use of crêpe weave. Printed silk crêpe florals (often from Liberty) were made into fashionable bias-cut summer dresses in the 1930s.

DAMASK A woven fabric in which the pattern is formed by the contrast of shiny warp face areas and matt weft face areas.

DOUBLE CLOTH Two 'cloths' which are woven on one loom simultaneously. Each 'cloth' has its own set of warps and wefts and they are connected during weaving only at points of interchange. A reversible fabric.

DUPLEX-PRINTING The same pattern is roller-printed or screen-printed on both sides of the fabric, which is thus reversible.

GLAZED COTTON Cotton which has a shiny surface which is achieved by various chemical or physical finishing processes. Many cottons lose this sheen when laundered.

JACQUARD A system of weaving elaborate patterns invented by Joseph-Marie Jacquard (1752-1834). By the mid-1820s jacquards started to be used in England but did not become widespread until the 1840s and 1850s. The jacquard mechanism uses a series of perforated cards to regulate which warp threads are lifted and which are lowered to form the design.

MOQUETTE Heavy duty upholstery fabric. It has a warp pile structure similar to Brussels carpet and velvet. The pile can be cut or uncut. Usually in woollen pile on cotton ground.

PLUSH Generic term for a cut pile fabric with a less dense and longer pile than velvet. Commonly a woollen pile on a cotton ground.

RAYON Name adopted to replace 'artificial silk' as the generic term for man-made fibres made from a cellulose base. The term was invented in America, where it was gradually accepted, and after 1925 it began to be used in Great Britain.

In 1928 it was officially adopted by Courtaulds. The two main types are viscose rayon and acetate. Viscose has the oldest history, but although it was patented in 1892 rapid expansion and mass production took place from about 1922 to 1930.

ROLLER-PRINTING A patent was taken out by Thomas Bell in 1783, but rapid technological development and large-scale exploitation took place in the 19th and 20th centuries. The design is engraved on copper rollers (one for each colour) which revolve around a central stationary roller. The engraving is filled with colour and the cloth pressed on to it. The entire width of the cloth is printed. Best-selling designs are usually roller-printed, as the cost of engraving the rollers is high and large quantities of cloth have to be printed and sold to recoup initial outlay. A quick patterning technique – one machine can print thousands of yards in one day.

SATIN (i) A warp-faced weave which is constructed to give an unbroken, lustrous surface. The close warp covers the weft. (ii) A fabric made by satin weave. Originally satin was all silk but it is now made from silk, cotton, rayon and other fibres.

SCREEN-PRINTING Basically a development of the stencil technique which produces a coloured surface design by forcing colour paste through a screen (fine mesh stretched over a frame) on which the pattern has been masked out. Each colour has a separate screen. It became increasingly popular towards the end of the 1920s and during the 1930s, being suited to broad design effects current in the later 20th century and an economical method by which to print short runs. The early hand process has now largely given way to sophisticated fully automatic flat and rotary machines.

SHADOW CRETONNE Term used in the industry to describe a warp-printed cotton furnishing fabric. The warp is printed prior to weaving; then the parti-coloured threads are interwoven with a one colour weft. This breaks up the solidity of the colour mass and produces a soft colour outline. Such warp prints had a ready market in the early to mid-1930s.

TAFFETA A plain-weave silk cloth characterised by its stiff, crisp feel and lustrous surface.

VELVET A close, cut, warp-pile fabric. The cut ends of the fibre form the fabric surface. Originally the term was applied only to silk fabrics which were the most expensive on the market.

VELVETEEN A close cut, weft-pile fabric. The cut ends of the fibre form the fabric surface. Particularly popular for furnishings in the late 19th and 20th centuries.

VOILE Semi-transparent, lightweight, open textured plain-weave cloth (can be of silk, cotton or wool) made with hard twisted yarns and produced in dress and furnishing qualities.

WARP Yarns running the length of the cloth, usually stronger than the horizontal weft yarns.

WEFT Yarns which interlace at right-angles with the warp.

WORSTED A wool yarn, generally from a special breed of sheep, which is carded and then combed to give a smooth rather than a fluffy surface. It was often heavily glazed in the 18th and 19th centuries and was used extensively for high quality furnishings and costume.

Notes on Firms and Designers

BAKER, G. P. & J. LTD., London. Textile printers. Founded by the brothers George Percival and James Baker in 1884. George formed an important collection of historical textiles (mainly Persian and Indian) and many of these designs were adapted and block-printed for Bakers by Swaisland & Co. at Crayford. In 1893 they took over Swaislands. Famous for their 1890s Art Nouveau printed fabrics and skilled adaptations of historical designs. Now owned by Parker Knoll.

BARRON and LARCHER. Phyllis Barron (1890-1964), Dorothy Larcher (1884-1952). Textile designers and printers. Phyllis Barron acquired a miscellaneous collection of French printing blocks and began experiments in textile printing and block cutting using 18th and 19th century handbooks. Early in the 1920s she was joined by the painter Dorothy Larcher. In 1930 both moved to Painswick, Gloucestershire and continued to print furnishing and dress fabrics. Commissions included furnishings for the Duke of Westminster's yacht *The Flying Cloud* and for the Senior Common Room, Girton College. In 1939 due to lack of materials and markets they were forced to stop printing. Phyllis Barron returned to painting flower studies. The Crafts Study Centre, University of Bath, has an extensive collection of their textiles.

BELL, VANESSA 1879-1961. Painter and designer. From 1913 to 1919 co-ordinator of The Omega Workshops, for which she designed textiles, pottery etc. In the 1920s and 1930s collaborated with Duncan Grant in the production of many interior schemes. Supplied Allan Walton with designs for screen-printed fabrics throughout the 1930s .

BROWN, F. GREGORY 1887-1948. Commercial artist and textile designer. From 1920 onwards he designed textiles for W. Foxton Ltd. and was awarded a gold medal for his textiles at the Paris Exhibition, 1925. Founder member of the Design and Industries Association.

CALICO PRINTERS' ASSOCIATION, Manchester. An amalgamation of 46 printing firms (several with spinning, weaving and dyeing plants), forming 85% of the British calico printing industry. It was established on November 8th, 1899.

CHRISTIE, MRS A. G. I. Embroideress, teacher and authoress. Stressed the importance of technically perfect hand stitchery. First teacher of embroidery The Royal College of Art. Wrote *Embroidery and Tapestry Weaving* (1906), *Samplers and Stitches* (1921) and *English Medieval Embroidery* (1938). Edited the magazines *Needle and Thread* and *Embroidery*.

COURTAULDS LTD. In 1816 Bocking silk mill was run by Samuel Courtauld (1793-1881), the principal founder. Courtaulds Ltd was incorporated in 1913. Famed for the production of crape and pioneers in the manufacture of rayon by the viscose process. In 1939, in conjunction with ICI, began production of nylon yarn. By 1940, together with its associated companies, it was one of the world's largest textile concerns.

CROMPTON, REBECCA 1894-1947. Embroideress. After training with Dorothy Benson at the Singer Sewing Machine Workroom she became a leading exponent of free, creative machine embroidery, often used in conjunction with hand techniques. Teacher and examiner of embroidery; wrote *Modern Design in Embroidery*, 1936.

CRYSEDE LTD., St. Ives, Cornwall. Textile printers. Started by Alec Walker in 1925. He produced designs for hand block-printed silk lengths, which were made up into dresses in the works. Tom Heron, who later founded the firm Cresta, was Managing Director of Crysede from 1926 to 1929.

DOBSON, FRANK 1888-1963. Sculptor and designer. Trained as a painter but established himself as a leading British sculptor. Designed and executed resist-printed textiles in the 1920s. Designed for commercial screen-printed soft furnishings (Allan Walton Textiles) as well as lino block-printing his own fabrics throughout the 1930s. 1946-53 Professor of Sculpture at The Royal College of Art.

DONALD BROTHERS LTD., Dundee. In 1936 described as the manufacturers of "Old Glamis Fabrics", with specialities listed as Art canvas, Art linens, and other decorative fabrics for Wall-hanging, Stencilling, Embroidering, Draping, Upholstering, etc. Best known for high quality woven linen furnishings .

DORN, MARION 1899-1964. Textile and carpet designer. Born and educated in San Francisco and came to England in the early 1920s. By the mid-1930s was generally acclaimed as a leading free-lance textile designer. In 1934 founded her own firm, Marion Dorn Ltd. In 1940 returned to USA. Re-established her career with difficulty in New York, but was only moderately successful.

EDINBURGH WEAVERS, Carlisle. Experimental designing and marketing unit of Morton Sundour Fabrics Ltd. Established originally in Edinburgh (1929), it was merged with the main weaving factory in 1930. Successfully directed by Alastair Morton, it issued avant-garde furnishings. Taken over by Courtaulds in 1963.

L'EXPOSITION INTERNATIONALE DES ARTS DÉCORATIFS ET INDUSTRIELS MODERNES, Paris, 1925. Originally planned in 1913, but delayed because of World War I. Covered a broad spectrum of contemporary decorative and industrial art. Reproductions and copies were forbidden. It occupied a vast and impressive site: the Grand Palais, the Cours La Reine, the Pont Alexandre III and the Esplanade des Invalides. The exhibition revealed the supremacy of French designers and manufacturers in many of the applied arts.

L'EXPOSITION INTERNATIONALE DES ARTS ET TECHNIQUES DAN LA VIE MODERNE, Paris, 1937. This extended over an even larger site than the 1925 Paris Exhibition. Its aim was "to demonstrate that the artistic concern with the details of daily existence can enhance the life of everyone, whatever their social condition; that no incompatibility exists between Usefulness and Beauty and that Art and Technology should be indissolubly linked". However, it was not as successful as the 1925 Exhibition.

FIRTH, T. F. & SONS LTD., Brighouse and Heckmondwike. Established in 1822 by Edwin Firth. Incorporated in 1889. In 1936 was producing Axminster, Wilton, Brussels, velvet and tapestry carpets (at Brighouse) and seamless Axminister squares, a wide variety of rugs, mantle cloths and furniture velvets, etc. (at Heckmondwike).

FOXTON, WILLIAM 1861-1945. Textile manufacturer. His firm, William Foxton, was founded in 1903 and known as W. Foxton Ltd. after 1923. Produced some of the most interesting artist-designed printed and woven furnishings of the 1920s and although no longer in the forefront during the 1930s issued many quality designs. The firm's records were destroyed during the blitz.

FRASER, CLAUD LOVAT 1890-1921. Painter, illustrator, theatre and textile designer. Favoured bold bright patterns, some of which were issued as printed furnishings by W. Foxton. His wife, Grace Lovat Fraser, became a consultant to the cotton industry and in 1948 she wrote *Textiles By Britain*.

FRY, ROGER 1866-1934. Painter, art critic, historian, lecturer and curator. 1905-10 was curator of paintings at the Metropolitan Museum, New York. Turned down offers of the directorships of the National Gallery (1905) and the Tate Gallery (1911). Organised two highly significant exhibitions of modern art in London at the Grafton galleries, 1910-11 *Manet and the Post-Impressionists* and 1912-13 *Second Post-Impressionist Exhibition of English, French and Russian Artists.* Founded The Omega Workshops Ltd. in 1913; they closed in June 1919. In 1933 appointed Slade Professor of Fine Art at Cambridge.

GRAFTON, F W & CO. In 1855 the founder, F. W. Grafton, took over Broad Oak Printworks, Accrington. The firm became part of the Calico Printers' Association in 1899. During the 1920s it specialised in printed voiles, as well as printing a variety of other dress and furnishing fabrics.

GRANT, DUNCAN 1885-1978. Painter and designer. In 1913 designed textiles, pottery, etc. for the Omega Workshops Ltd. In 1920s and 1930s collaborated with Vanessa Bell in the production of interior schemes, many completed by rugs, printed furnishings and embroideries. His designs for printed textiles were produced by Allan Walton.

HAVINDEN, ASHLEY 1903-73.   Graphic artist, textile designer and abstract painter. In 1922 he joined the advertising agency W. S. Crawford and by 1960 was its Vice-Chairman. He had many influential clients for his advertising work. In 1933 he began designing rugs and textiles for leading British manufacturers.

HOGARTH, MARY HENRIETTA UPPLEBY 1862-1935.   Painter, embroideress and teacher. A supporter of the avant-garde, she encouraged artists to design embroideries and herself executed designs by Duncan Grant and Wyndham Tryon. Staunch supporter and official of the Embroiderers Guild.

KAUFFER, EDWARD McKNIGHT 1890-1954.   Graphic artist and theatre designer. Born and educated in the USA; trained as a painter and came to England in 1914. Received important commissions for his graphic work. He illustrated a number of books and designed rugs for The Wilton Royal Carpet Factory.

KING JESSIE MARION 1876-1949.   Illustrator, painter, designer, book binder and textile printer. Trained at Glasgow School of Art. Known especially for her linear book illustrations. Designed printed textiles for commercial manufacture (some sold by Liberty) as well as producing her own resist-printed (batik) fabrics. Wrote a handbook on this art – *How Cinderella was able to go to the ball*, 1924.

LEE, ARTHUR H. & SONS LTD., Birkenhead, Lancashire. Textile weavers, printers and embroiderers. Established by Arthur H. Lee in 1888. Started in Warrington; removed to Birkenhead in 1908. Produced some significant Art Nouveau fabrics by leading designers in the 1890s and early 1900s, but thereafter specialised in reproduction woven fabrics and embroideries for furnishing and upholstery. Agent for textiles printed by Mariano Fortuny in Venice. The firm was dissolved and assets sold in 1972.

LIBERTY & CO. LTD., London.   Founded in 1875 by Arthur Lasenby Liberty. Started as an importer of Eastern goods, but expanded rapidly to sell home manufactured furniture, metalwork, dress, ceramics and fabrics under the Liberty name. Especially well known for their Art Nouveau textiles and floral dress fabrics (still produced). Many of their fabrics were printed and woven by outside firms but in 1904 they took over E Littler's printworks at Merton Abbey and here they block-printed and later screen-printed their own textiles until 1973. The present design studio of Liberty of London Prints Ltd is near this original Merton Abbey site.

MACKINTOSH, CHARLES RENNIE 1868-1928. Architect, water-colourist and designer of furniture, metalwork and textiles. Trained at Glasgow School of Art. Probably his most famous buildings are the Glasgow School of Art, Miss Cranston's tearooms and Hill House. From 1916 to 1923 he lived in Chelsea and during these years designed many textiles, some of which were printed by W. Foxton Ltd. and Seftons.

MAROMME PRINTWORKS.   Printers of French cretonnes, delaine, silk and flannel Printworks at Rouen, France. London headquarters at 6 Snow Hill, EC1. Roger Fry contracted them to print linens for his Omega Workshops by a special technique involving rollers – possibly surface printing.

MAWSON, SYDNEY.   Textile and wallpaper designer. A versatile artist with a wide stylistic range. In the 1890s his work was greatly influenced by William Morris's patterns. By the early 1900s he produced bold designs with huge repeats. After about 1905 he specialised in finely drawn naturalistic patterns and in the 1920s, inspired by Persian art, he designed best-selling garden scenes for Morton Sundour's roller-prints.

McLEISH, MINNIE 1876-1957.   Textile designer. In the 1920s she worked in a free-lance capacity for a number of firms, but especially for W. Foxton Ltd. Her forte was bold brightly coloured patterns for printed furnishings.

MERTON ABBEY.   Workshops on the banks of the river Wandle between Wandsworth and Wimbledon, built on the site of a medieval abbey. Used by silk and cotton dyers and printers in the 18th and 19th centuries, due to the availability of soft water. Morris and Company took over a disused 18th century silk-dyeing works in 1881 and produced woven and printed textiles, tapestries, embroideries and stained glass there until 1940. In 1904 Libertys took over another works on the site that was previously used by E. Littler, the block printers, who had produced many of Liberty's printed silks until this date.

MORTON, ALEXANDER & CO., Darvel and Carlisle. Established as a madras weaving firm by Alexander Morton (1844-1921), at Darvel, Ayrshire. Alexander Morton introduced power-driven lace machines and achieved great success. In 1890 he started to manufacture carpets – the Donegal carpets hand-knotted in Ireland were famous. Alexander's second son, James (1867-1943), joined the firm and during the late 19th and 20th century encouraged the production of adventurous designs by leading designers (C. F. A. Voysey, L. P. Butterfield, etc.). In 1900 transfer of operations to the Carlisle site began and by 1914 only lace and madras production remained at Darvel. In 1904-05 fabrics were printed for them by other firms but in 1912 they set up their own hand block-printing unit (under Morton Sundour roller-printing began in 1921 and screen-printing in 1931). In 1914 nearly all Alexander Morton's production, except for lace and carpet factories, was taken over by Morton Sundour Fabrics, directed by James Morton.

MORTON SUNDOUR FABRICS LTD, Carlisle, etc. Textile manufacturers. Formed in 1914 with James Morton (1867-1943) as Governing Director. It took over nearly all the manufactories, save for lace and carpet production, of Alexander Morton & Co. Specialised in 'Sundour' unfadable fabrics. After 1914 researched and manufactured synthetic vat dyestuffs. Under James Morton's energetic direction the firm produced well designed reliable fabrics (including a wide range of woven fabrics) at reasonable cost.

NASH, PAUL 1889-1946. Painter, graphic artist and designer of textiles, glass, and china. His first textile designs were hand-printed 1925-29 by Mrs Eric Kennington at her workshop 'Footprints'. He encouraged Miss E. A. Little's venture, 'Modern Textiles', a shop which sold high quality crafts including fabrics. He designed dress fabrics for Tom Heron's firm Cresta Silks Ltd., upholstery for London Transport and furnishings for Old Bleach Linen Co.

NICHOLSON, BEN 1894-1982. Painter. Also designed textiles. In 1934 with Barbara Hepworth exhibited hand-printed textiles and rugs. Some of his fabric designs were lino blockprinted by Nancy Nicholson at the Poulk Press. In 1937 he collaborated with Alastair Morton (Edinburgh Weavers) to produce the range of 'Constructivist Fabrics'. In 1948 he designed for Zika Ascher's limited editions of screen-printed silk squares.

OLD-BLEACH LINEN COMPANY LTD., Randalstown, Northern Ireland. Linen manufacturers, bleachers and merchants. Established in 1870 by C. J. Webb . Produced embroidery, dress and furnishing linens, damask table linens and embroidered goods. Published *The Embroideress* in conjunction with James Pearsall & Co. Ltd., manufacturers of embroidery yarns, knitting wools, etc.

THE OMEGA WORKSHOPS LTD., 33 Fitzroy Square, Soho, London. Founded in 1913 by Roger Fry as a group of artists designing furniture, pottery, carpets, textiles, stained glass and whole schemes of interior decoration (Cadena Cafe, a room at the Daily Mail's Ideal Home Exhibition 1913, a lounge at the Allied Artist's Exhibition 1914, etc.). The artists included Vanessa Bell, Duncan Grant, Frederick Etchells, Nina Hamnett, etc. The outbreak of war hindered the venture as artists left to join the war effort and production declined. In 1919 the Workshops were closed.

SANDERSON, ARTHUR & SONS LTD. Wallpaper and textile manufacturers. Established in 1860 by Arthur Sanderson (d. 1882), incorporated in 1900. The furnishing fabric printworks were built at Uxbridge in 1921 and weaving started here in 1934.

SCOTT, MACKAY HUGH BAILLIE 1865-1945. Architect and designer. Built houses in Europe and USA, many complete with his furnishings (furniture, metalwork and textiles). His first textiles were designed in the late 1880s. In the early 1900s he designed embroideries, executed by his wife, and woven and printed furnishings.

SHERINGHAM, GEORGE 1884-1937. Decorative painter, theatrical designer, book illustrator, fan and textile designer.

Trained as a painter. Designed scenery and costumes for a number of plays and operas. Produced many watercolour designs for fans. Supplied Seftons with patterns for printed furnishing and dress fabrics, as well as designs for silk handkerchiefs .

SILVER STUDIO. Founded by Arthur Silver in 1880 for the production of repeating designs for wallpapers and textiles and designs for silverwork. On his death, his son Rex took over the firm, concentrating on silver designs, with Harry Napper organising the production of wallpaper and textile designs. The Studio sold designs to a number of manufacturers and directly to shops, especially Libertys, who had the designs manufactured under their own label.

SIMPSON, RONALD D. 1890-1960. Textile designer and woodworker of Kendal. Joined Alexander Morton & Co. in 1908 and produced many designs for the firm's printed ranges, as well as amusing advertisements for their unfadable 'Sundour' fabrics.

STEAD MCALPIN & COMPANY LTD. Founded in 1745 by Kenneth McAlpin with a dye-works at Wigton in Cumberland; later took over the local printworks. Moved to empty premises of a calico printworks at Cummersdale, the site of the present works. Won gold medal at the 1862 Exhibition. One of the earliest firms to produce glazed chintzes by engraved copper rollers. Block-printing continued until 1978. Produces prints for Libertys and John Lewis.

STEINER, F & CO. LTD., Church, near Accrington, Lancashire. Dyers and calico printers. Frederick Steiner, a chemist, came to Britain in the early 19th century, took over Church printworks (founded in 1722) in the 1840s and acquired other works in the area. The firm were high quality printers who used top designers and issued important Art Nouveau fabrics. Remained independent when many similar Lancashire firms joined the Calico Printers' Association Ltd. in 1899. Went into voluntary liquidation in 1955.

TOOTAL BROADHURST LEE CO. LTD., Manchester. Textile manufacturers and merchants. Established in the early part of the 19th century as Atkinson, Tootal & Co. Specialised in high quality fancy white and dyed cotton and silk goods. Today the firm has extensive plant in Lancashire and trades as Tootal Fabrics Ltd.

TURNBULL & STOCKDALE LTD., Ramsbottom, Lancashire. Textile printers, dyers, bleachers and finishers. Established in 1881. In the same year Lewis F. Day was appointed the firm's Art Director. Their hand block-printed textiles are some of the most interesting of the late 19th and early 20th century. They are now one of the few surviving hand block-printers in Great Britain.

VOYSEY C. F. A. 1857-1941. Architect and designer of textiles, wallpapers, furniture, metalwork and ceramics. He set up in architectural practice in 1882 and began designing textiles under the guidance of A. H. Mackmurdo. Member of the Art Workers Guild (Master in 1924) and the Arts and Crafts Exhibition Society. Wrote on economic theories as related to the decorative arts. He had great influence on British contemporaries and on the European Art Nouveau school. His printed textile designs were produced by Stead McAlpin, Wylie and Lockhead, Newman, Smith and Newman, G. P. & J. Baker, Morton Sundour Fabrics, Muntzer & Co. Woven textiles were manufactured by Alexander Morton & Co., A. H. Lee & Sons. Carpets were woven by Tomkinson & Adam, Yates & Co. and possibly Templeton & Co.

WALKER, ALEC GEORGE. Learnt weaving, dyeing and finishing processes in his family's mill in Yorkshire. In 1925, set up his own works (Crysede Silks) at Newlyn, Cornwall (slightly later it moved to St Ives). He designed most of the dress prints for the firm.

WALTON, ALLAN 1891-1948. Textile designer and manufacturer interior decorator. Trained as an architect, then as a painter. As Director of Allan Walton Textiles he commissioned some of the most enterprising artist-designed screen-printed fabrics of the 1930s. From 1943 to 1945 he was Director of the Glasgow School of Art.

94 WARNER & SONS LTD. Leading 19th and 20th century silk weavers and cotton printers. Founded by Benjamin Warner, who trained at the Spitalfields School of Design, the firm has worked under the following names: Warner, Sillett & Ramm (before 1875), Warner & Ramm (1875-92), Warner & Sons (1892 onwards).

In the later 19th century the firm took over the goodwill, plant and designs of various firms such as Daniel Walters & Co. and Charles Norris (formerly Keith & Co.). The first workshops were in Spitalfields, but in 1873 larger premises were taken at Hollybush Gardens, Bethnal Green. Later, the whole weaving operation was transferred to Braintree Mills in Essex; the printing works were at Dartford, Kent (the premises of Newman, Smith and Newman, a firm absorbed by Warners).

Warners were noted for high technical achievements and good design. They employed all the leading designers of the day for furnishing and dress fabrics. In 1936 they advertised as 'Weavers of Silks, Velvets and other Furnishing Fabrics; Printers of Linens and Chintzes and Upholsterers' Warehousemen... Specialists in the reproduction of old documents and fabrics in contemporary design.'

Alec Hunter joined the firm in 1932; as production manager he controlled the style and design of their output until 1958. He gave invaluable advice to free-lance designers about yarns and cloth construction and encouraged experiments for powerloom production of modern designs.

THE WILTON ROYAL CARPET FACTORY LTD., Wilton, near Salisbury. Carpet and rug manufacturers, established in the early 18th century. Leading 19th century producers of pile carpets; worked under contract for Morris and Company, etc. In 1934 they listed Wilton, Brussels and Axminster carpets as their specialities. During the 1930s they produced Wessex hand-tufted rugs, designed by leading artists. The firm still flourishes, but the hand looms no longer operate.

RECOMMENDED READING

The titles were published in London unless otherwise stated

ANSCOMBE, A. *Omega and After: Bloomsbury and the Decorative Arts*, Thames and Hudson, 1981

BATTERSBY, M. *The Decorative Twenties*, Studio Vista, 1969

BATTERSBY, M. *The Decorative Thirties*, Studio Vista, 1971

BILLCLIFFE, R. *Mackintosh Textile Designs*, John Murray, 1982

COLEMAN, D. C. *Courtaulds: An Economic and Social History*, Oxford University Press, Oxford, 1969

COLLINS J. *The Omega Workshops*, Secker and Warburg, 1984

GOODDEN, S. *A History of Heal's*, Heal and Son Ltd., 1984

HAYES MARSHALL, H. G. *British Textile Designers Today*, F Lewis, Leigh-on-Sea, 1939

LEWIS, F. (ed.) *British Designers and their Work*, F. Lewis, Leigh-on-Sea, 1941

LOVAT FRASER, G. *Textiles by Britain*, Allen & Unwin, 1948

HEALS *Heals Catalogues 1835-1934*, David and Charles, Newton Abbott, 1972

HINCHCLIFFE, F. *Thirties Floral Fabrics*, Webb and Bower, 1988

HUNT, A. *Textile Design*, Studio, 1937

KING, JESSIE MARION *How Cinderella was able to go to the ball*, Foulis, 1924

MACCARTHY, F. *British Design Since 1880*, Lund Humphries, 1982

MENDES, V. *Novelty Fabrics*, Webb and Bower, 1988

MORTON J. W. F. *Three Generations in a Family Textile Firm*, Routledge & Kegan Paul, 1971

NEWMAN G. and FORTY, A. *British Design. A Survey of Design in Britain 1915-1939. The Electric Home*, Open University Press, 1975

PARRY, L. *Textiles of the Arts and Crafts Movement*, Thames and Hudson, 1988

PEVSNER, N. *An Enquiry into Industrial Art in England*, Cambridge University Press, Cambridge 1973

SCHOESER, M. *Fabrics and Wallpapers: Twentieth Century Design*, Unwin Hyman, 1986

SCHOESER, M. and RUFEY, C. *English and American Textiles from 1790 to the Present*, Thames and Hudson, 1989

STOREY, J. *Textile Printing*, Thames and Hudson, 1974

STORY, J. *Dyes and Fabrics*, Thames and Hudson, 1978

TURNBULL, G. *A History of the Calico Printing Industry*, John Sherratt & Son, Altrincham

EXHIBITION CATALOGUES

Bath, Crafts Study Centre, Holburne Museum, *Hand block printed Textiles. Phyllis Barron and Dorothy Larcher*, 1978

Braintree, Bury, H. *A Choice of Design 1850-1980. Fabrics by Warner & Sons Ltd.*, Warner & Sons Ltd., 1981

Braintree, Shoeser, M. *Fifties Printed Textiles*, Warner & Sons Ltd., 1985

Brighton, The Royal Pavilion and Museum, *British Carpets and Designs: The Modernist Rug 1928-1938*, 1975

Edinburgh, The Scottish Gallery of Modern Art, *Alastair Morton and Edinburgh Weavers*, 1978

London, Arts Council and the Victoria and Albert Museum, *Thirties. British Art and Design Before the War*, 1979

London, The Camden Arts Centre, *Enid Marx. A Retrospective Exhibition*, 1979

London, Victoria and Albert Museum, *Catalogue of a Loan Exhibition of English Chintz*, 1960

London, Victoria and Albert Museum, *A Century of Warner Fabrics 1870 to 1970*, 1973

London, Victoria and Albert Museum, *The Mortons: Three Generations of Textile Creation*, 1973

London, Victoria and Albert Museum, *Liberty's 1875-1975 An exhibition to mark the firm's centenary*, 1975

London, Victoria and Albert Museum, *Paul Nash as Designer*, 1975

London, Victoria and Albert Museum, *From East to West: Textiles from G. P. & J. Baker*, G. P. & J. Baker, 1984

London, Woods, C. *Sanderson's 1860-1985*, Arthur Sanderson & Sons Ltd. 1985

Manchester, The Whitworth Art Gallery, *Modern Art in Textile Design*, 1963